Advance Praise for *Cyber Rules*

"In *Cyber Rules,* Thomas Siebel and Pat House define the new rules of E-business, blueprinting how organizations will market to, sell, and service their customers."
  —**Eckhard Pfeiffer, President and CEO, Compaq Computer Corporation**

"A first-hand, insightful vision of e-commerce's future. Their technological sophistication notwithstanding, the authors keep the spotlight where it belongs—on the satisfied customer."
  —**Dan Case, Chairman and CEO, Hambrecht & Quist**

"If you are exploring the use of electronic channels, whether you're already Internet-fluent or just getting started, *Cyber Rules* is mandatory reading before you go any further."
  —**Scott Hartz, Global Managing Partner, PricewaterhouseCoopers Management Consulting Services**

"The Internet, everyone knows by now, will change business fundamentals forever. Funny, though—one thing will never change. Winners will always outmarket and outsell their competition. Tom Siebel and Pat House give you the expert's guide to the future."
  —**Rich Karlgaard, Publisher, *Forbes Magazine***

"Charts the opportunities and the pitfalls of the rapidly digitizing economy. Web veteran or Web novice, if you're concerned about online channels, you need this book."
  —**Dr. Friedrich Froeschl, President and CEO, Siemens Business Services GmbH & Co. OHG**

"The Internet makes possible, for the first time in history, a fully distributed yet fully connected sales and marketing model. *Cyber Rules* is essential reading for anyone interested in understanding and implementing that model."
  —**Richard G. Sherlund, Managing Director, Goldman, Sachs & Co.**

Cyber Rules

Strategies for Excelling at E-Business

Thomas M. Siebel
and Pat House

Currency/Doubleday

New York

London

Toronto

Sydney

Auckland

A Currency Book

PUBLISHED BY DOUBLEDAY

a division of Random House, Inc.

1540 Broadway, New York, New York 10036

Currency and Doubleday are trademarks of Doubleday,

a division of Random House, Inc.

Book design by Chris Welch

Library of Congress Cataloging-in-Publication Data

Siebel, Thomas M.

Cyber Rules: Strategies for Excelling at E-Business

Thomas M. Siebel and Pat House.

p.   cm.

Includes index.

1. Electronic commerce.   2. Strategic management.   I. Title.

HF5548.32.S54   1999

658'.054678—dc21   98-51432

CIP

ISBN 0-385-49412-2

11 13 15 17 19 20 18 16 14 12

Contents

Part I: The First Five Years

Part II: On the Horizon: E-Business's Cyber Rules

Contents

Part III: Getting There from Here

Foreword

We're living in an incredible time, when high technology is playing an increasingly important and meaningful role in everyone's lives. The Internet, which is perhaps the most visible evidence of this phenomenon, has revolutionized the way people and companies communicate. Its growth has been explosive because it gives us tremendous access to information that makes our lives simpler to manage. This, in turn, has had a revolutionary impact on business.

Yet at the heart of E-business growth is an interesting paradox. As Tom Siebel and Pat House emphasize in this fascinating book, E-business has been built on technology, but it's not *about* technology. It's about the same thing that solid business growth has always been about: the satisfaction of individual customers' needs. That has been a single-minded commitment at our company and at their company, Siebel Systems, Inc.

I am often asked how the Internet has changed our business at Charles Schwab. The perhaps surprising answer is: "It really hasn't." Rather than fundamentally *changing* our business, the Internet has *enhanced* the way we have been operating since I founded the company back in 1971.

At that time, retail brokerage was dominated by old, entrenched banks, S&Ls, and brokerage companies. These institutions were so fixed in their ways that they had lost sight of their most important asset—the individual customer. If you wanted to make an investment, you could only do so according to your broker's schedule—and if you weren't a high-net-worth individual, you might have difficulty even getting your broker on the phone. At Schwab we were determined to make investing accessible and affordable for everyone by providing superior customer service, value pricing, multiple methods of access, a large array of investment choices, and a high degree of investor control.

The Internet has enhanced our achievement of this mission by making online services both cost-effective and accessible to everyone, anywhere, at any time. At Charles Schwab we've actually been offering online capabilities to our customers for nearly ten years. Today, with everyone becoming Internet-savvy, we have more than 1.9 million online accounts transacting $2 billion every week, and we receive over 50 percent of our customer orders through online channels.

But this success has been *enabled* by technology, not caused by it. We have grown on the Internet because we have looked at this dramatic new communications medium strategically, as a natural extension of our core business. We've always tried to empower investors. Now we're able to combine the Internet's speed of delivery, low cost, and global presence with our continuing off-line customer service channels. The Internet provides us a powerful outlet to strengthen our commitment to customer satisfaction.

A parallel philosophy is in place at Siebel Systems. Tom Siebel and Pat House not only understand how to leverage Internet technology, but they are committed to doing whatever it takes to make their customers successful. Pioneers in enterprise relationship management and its enabling technologies, they have created a software company that is dedicated to bringing the power of information to building customer relationships. This makes it a natural leader in the world of E-business.

In *Cyber Rules,* Tom and Pat offer an insider's perspective on the underlying principles of E-business and highlight the key risks and opportunities in this exciting new arena. They also give us a glimpse into the fast-approaching future of the Internet. They envision a world in which the Internet affects literally everything about the way we do business and, as such, impacts all our lives. Yet they powerfully remind the reader that this transformation will only happen for companies that focus on service to the individual customer—every business organization's most important asset.

That's something that the experiences of both our companies consistently demonstrate, and to which I, as an Internet early adopter, can thoroughly relate. I hope you learn from and enjoy this book as much as I did.

—Charles R. Schwab
Founder and Chairman
The Charles Schwab Corporation

Cyber Rules

The Digital Watershed

Every so often an event occurs that is so startling in its economic implications that it may reasonably be considered a watershed in the way we do business. By "watershed" we mean an abrupt and irrevocable turning point, one that signals a shift in historical direction by obliterating an established set of business practices and replacing them with a new commercial paradigm. We are in the initial stages of such a watershed now, with the meteoric rise to prominence of the World Wide Web.

The advent of the Web was an unprecedented event that has already begun to set us on a path that will radically alter how we interact not only with computers, but with one another, with institutions both private and public, and with business associates and customers around the globe. In the online world of the very near future, the Internet will link every home, every business, every government agency, and every distributed database together in a complex weave of information exchange. We will inhabit a world where distance no longer matters, and where communication and data transfer will be virtually instantaneous. This will so thoroughly transform the way that transactions are conducted that doing business *without* the Web will become unthinkable.

There have been other watersheds of this magnitude, but not many—maybe ten or twenty in the span of business history. The first, perhaps, was the invention of writing, which enabled grain merchants in ancient Mesopotamia to rationalize their inventory. A second was the appearance of metal currency—that dramatic attack on the barter system that occurred in Lydia, on the eastern Mediterranean, several thousand years ago. Subsequent watersheds would include the adoption of the Arabic zero, double-entry bookkeeping, and joint stock ownership. All of them transformed the shape of commercial enterprise.

The Internet is doing the same thing, only quicker. The speed with which it is reaching watershed magnitude gives it a possibly unique status in economic history. We're not speaking about the speed of data transmission that is one of its rightful claims to fame, but the speed with which businesses have picked up on the Internet's potential, have adopted its technology, and are staking successful claims on this economic frontier. That speed is causing investment counselors who were scoffing at Internet businesses only two or three years ago to call them the current miracles of the world's stock exchanges. No previous watershed has elicited such a rush to approval.

Although the Internet as a military experiment had been around since the 1960s, its business potential was broached only

in 1993, when the first commercial Web sites began to be deployed. That's only a few years ago, and yet the Net has already
made a quantum leap from a technological curiosity to the story
of the century. Thus the Net is presenting itself as a watershed
with virtually no lag time. It seems to have sprung, like Athena,
from some cybergod's brow, fully clothed and fully armed. That
perception is somewhat illusory, as you'll discover, but it's a perception that has to be dealt with as if it were true, because it is
generating a mind-boggling market revolution that is already di-
viding the world into "Netizens" and "Netwits."

You think "mind-boggling" is too strong a term? Consider
these statistics from leading technology industry analysts.

- According to the Parallax group, in 1998 an estimated 30 million American households owned computers, and probably
  half of them had modem capabilities. Both figures were expected to double by the end of the century.
- Find/SVP Inc. estimates that the number of regular Web users
  jumped from 8.4 million in 1996 to 28 million two years later. By
  the year 2000, the number was expected to exceed 200 million.
- The U.S. Department of Commerce gives an even more startling
  estimate. Its recent study *The Emerging Digital Economy* identifies over 60 million U.S. Web users today, with another 40 million overseas. Their projection for the year 2005 is 1 billion users.
- A recent survey by the Graphic, Visualization, and Usability
  Center at Georgia Tech University gave average Web user income as $63,000, with over 10 percent reporting income of
  over $100,000. BancAmerica estimates that these users' aver-
  age per-person annual Web expenditure of $24 will quadruple
  by the end of the century.

- The hype of "infotainment" aside, Internet usage has an unmistakable business orientation. Response Analysis Corporation found that a majority of online households have an in-home office.
- The presence of larger businesses may be gauged by the upsurge in registered domain names, from 26,000 in 1993 to over 1.5 million today. New commercial sites are being added to the World Wide Web at the rate of about 5,000 a month. That's one new place of business every nine minutes.
- Forrester Research estimates that, in 1997, online transactions amounted to $9 billion; of that figure, the bulk—$7.5 billion— was in business-to-business sales. One leader in this field, Cisco Systems, Inc., brought in online revenues of $3.2 billion. The Commerce Department projects $300 billion in business-to-business sales by the year 2002.
- Between 1995 and 1997, according to a Price Waterhouse study, annual venture capital funding for online businesses went from $134 million to $1.88 billion.

And there's a small coda to this final point. While venture capitalists continue to favor more traditional recipients—especially firms in the communications and general software sectors—the Net is fast coming on as an arena of "high drama." Beginning from a smidgen of support in 1995, E-business in 1997 commanded 14 percent of the funding total.

Impressive figures. But if you want to get an even more impressive feel for the new medium's potential, look at these already galloping Net statistics as examples not of simple growth but of *untapped potential.*

Consider, for example, the fact that those 30 million wired

households represent only a fraction of total North American households. Or the fact, according to the *Nielsen Internet Demographics Survey*, that the $9 billion of online transactions were generated by only 14 percent of Web users. Or the most sobering (or is it stimulating?) fact of all: that electronic business, however explosive, still accounts for only a tiny proportion of our GNP. Jupiter Communications notes that, in 1997, when the Net registered that soaring $9 billion in sales, print-based catalog sales were edging toward $70 billion, and the retail take as a whole was over $2 trillion.

So the growth of Net business is exhilarating, but it's got a long way to go. We are sitting, right now, on the edge of a vast goldfield, and the riches it will one day surrender are only beginning to be revealed.

We're using the goldfield analogy for a double purpose. It should make you justifiably excited—but also cautious. For while millions are there for the making in the field of E-business, they are certainly not there for the taking, like picking nuggets off the ground. Anyone contemplating doing business on the World Wide Web might profit from remembering the lessons of that classic gold-hunting story *The Treasure of the Sierra Madre*.

In John Huston's great film, the novice prospector Fred C. Dobbs, played by Humphrey Bogart, enters his field of dreams with unbridled optimism, imagining that gold will jump from the ground into his pockets. Once he's out in the digs, reality sets in, and he discovers that making a fortune is not automatic. It demands a mixture of judgment, patience, and sweat—and, not least of all, cooperation with good partners to protect yourself from natural disasters and bandits.

Those lessons are directly applicable to the goldfield of the

Net. To excel at E-business, you need dedication, good partners, a sound business proposition—and maybe a little bit of luck. We can't help you with the luck, but we can help you with the rest. That's why we wrote this book. It's a brief and practical guide to scoping out the electronic goldfield, to learning how to survive in this radically new environment so that you can avoid the bandits and build a secure and profitable business enterprise.

Radically new. The point is central. Even though E-business is still business, the electronic "market space" that the Net has created operates under a dual set of rules. One set you already know, or you wouldn't be in business: It involves time-tested principles like identifying target markets, assessing and meeting your customers' needs, providing reliable service, and so on. The other set is no less important, but it's less familiar and—like all watershed rules—less commonsensical. In fact, many of the "cyber rules" of this developing environment seem to directly contradict established practices, and are therefore seen by traditional businesspeople as at the very least unusual.

Here's an example from a fascinating article by Kevin Kelly, executive editor of *Wired* magazine. In the emerging networked economy, Kelly writes, every increase in connectivity creates an increase in value. According to "the law of plenitude," the value of every individual fax machine goes up each time another fax machine is plugged in, because of the enhanced synergistic effect of greater information flow. But this notion flatly contradicts the industrial-age axiom that value comes from scarcity—the old "supply-demand" mantra. The challenge of E-business is to reconcile such novel ideas to the established business principles that we've been using for generations.

Eric Schmidt, who is the chairman and CEO of the software

leader Novell, puts an interesting spin on this point when he compares the relative importance of Moore's Law and Metcalf's Law. Moore's Law, which was defined by and named for Intel's Gordon Moore, says that computing capacity, as measured by the speed of microprocessors, doubles on average every eighteen months. That's a startling enough observation when you compare the eighteen-month estimate to, say, the doubling times for technology in heavy manufacturing. But, as Eric points out, an even more dramatic "law" is the one that was named for the founder of 3Com, Robert Metcalf.

Metcalf's Law, which is a modern version of the old law of increasing returns, says that the value of a network increases in direct proportion to the square of the number of machines that are on it. Is that a statistically verifiable law? No. But it's a good way of articulating an important message, the message of what we usually call the network effect. Kelly's law of plenitude is a version of the same thing. Whether the squaring principle is true or not mathematically isn't all that important, because the sense of it is true, with regard to positive returns.

Today, the most interesting rules have to do with these two principles: Moore's and Metcalf's laws. But Moore's Law is inherently limited by the nature of silicon. After a certain microprocessor gate size—around one micron, or a billionth of an inch—you can't get any more speed, so you reach a ceiling and Moore's Law ceases to have any effect. That will happen in another ten years, maybe a little longer. In the meantime, networks everywhere are growing dramatically, and this is having a much more important, exponential effect.

Eventually, in terms of how business is being conducted, the fact that my spreadsheet gets twice as fast every eighteen months is not nearly as interesting as the fact that my network is getting interconnected with those of my friends. That creates increasing returns that are more valuable than just more speed, so that eventually the network effect dominates Moore's Law.

As Eric's observation suggests, the key to the liberating power of any network—including the world's biggest network, the Internet—is the potential that it carries for total connectivity. In this book, we'll show you what doors that key can unlock without slipping into either technobabble or that semimystical enthusiasm for "connectivity" that has been called "Rapture of the Net." Actually, you don't need to be rapturous to be honestly enthusiastic. Once this watershed technology is fully embraced—and we're talking about years, not decades, for that to occur—it will completely transform the way that we think about business, and about how we must connect with our customers to keep ourselves profitable.

The heart of this transformation is "virtuality," or the ability to conduct transactions on a global level, in an instantaneous, or "real-time," format without having to consider the constraints of physical location. In the virtual world of E-business, *physical distance is irrelevant.* Which means that the time between inquiry and order is so compressed that, for all practical purposes, there is *no more waiting time.* This fact alone radically changes how customers are already shopping in cyberspace, how they will continue to shop, and how businesses must position themselves to keep their attention.

If you're a customer—and a customer here could mean an individual or a multinational corporation—virtuality means that, once you're online, you have a nearly infinite array of products and services available, a mouse click away. You can comparison shop nearly at light speed, even though one potential supplier might be in Honolulu and another in Vienna. You can order products that you have configured yourself, having them manufactured to your detailed specifications, and arrange for payment and delivery on the spot. And you can do all this in a paperless environment, from the comfort and convenience of your own home. The Internet, more than any previous technology, *empowers* the customer.

This has profound implications for business. If you're a business professional in the Internet age, you're confronting the fact that, virtually overnight, your potential customer base has exploded in size, the choices available to those customers have gone through the stratosphere, and hundreds of new competitors are suddenly grappling for their attention. In order to thrive in this world, you *must* be online.

The time to do that is now. "Going digital," in the digital age, is an imperative. It's not a means of ensuring subtle increments in operating margin. For all but the smallest, most local, mom-and-pop operations, learning how to excel at E-business is a matter of survival. We intend this book, therefore, as a general introduction to profiting in the electronic goldfield and to avoiding the mistakes that have already left it strewn with corporate corpses.

How, specifically, can you profit from *Cyber Rules*? The answer to that depends largely on who you are. To give you a better understanding of whether this book is for you, here's an overview:

Part I describes where we've gotten to so far. It surveys the first five years of electronic business, reviewing some of the arena's most famous success stories and providing a brief compendium of "first-generation" lessons. If your company is heavily committed to online commerce and you're already reasonably familiar with

Internet literature, you may want to skip this section and go directly to Part II. If you're a relative newcomer to E-business, if you're still weighing its potential before investing heavily, or if you just want a quick reminder of how we've gotten here, Part I will provide you a snapshot of the current situation.

Chapter 1 introduces the "virtual marketplace" that is the World Wide Web today. It demonstrates, based on the experiences of early adopters, what the business Internet is and what it's not. We'll review here the initial overblown claims about the medium and show how the Web's real potential is very different from what we once thought it was.

As exciting as it is, the world of E-business contains problems as well as opportunities. Chapter 2 addresses the two most commonly cited areas of concern among business professionals using the World Wide Web: the so-called bandwidth problem and issues of security.

Chapter 3 is a primer for doing business on the Net. In it, we lay out some basic principles to keep in mind before "going digital." These basics comprise a kind of map into the electronic goldfields, showing you the safest paths to travel and the ones to avoid.

In Part II we leave the immediate past and look toward the future. This section concentrates on trends that are only now emerging, but that will become increasingly important in the Internet's "second generation."

Chapter 4 focuses on the growing shift from the "infotainment" that has seemingly dominated the Internet so far to the global enterprise capabilities that are now bringing it to the next level. Chapter 5 explains how such online pioneers as Amazon.com and Preview Travel are destined to transform their entire industries—even though they may not remain those industries' leaders. Chapter 6 corrects a common "either-or" characterization by showing how traditional and online channels can provide complementary, rather than antagonistic, marketing possibilities.

Chapter 7 discusses the emergence of extended enterprises, or "para-enterprises," showing how the Internet has radically transformed traditional relationships between corporate entities, resellers, and end-use customers. Chapter 8 focuses on those end-use customers, showing how the Internet has empowered—and will continue to empower—them and has forced businesses to customize their products to serve "markets of one." Chapter 9 brings this lesson to its logical conclusion, by showing how the rise of Internet-based relationship management models will make "100 percent customer satisfaction" the benchmark of the future.

The third and final part of *Cyber Rules* is a practical guide to making a mark in E-business. Chapter 10, which is directed to managers in large businesses, outlines a digital strategy that can bring you bottom-line results. Chapter 11 is a corresponding discussion for smaller businesses: It shows how to get yourself connected, including the basics of how to maintain a profitable company Web site. We end the book, in Chapter 12, with a call to action—a final look at why excelling at E-business should be mission-critical for any business that intends to survive in the Web's next generation.

"Survive" is a strong word, and we're aware that to some observers it may sound extravagant. Many business professionals, alert to the Net's current limitations, are visibly unimpressed with the medium's promise. Some executives have been so slow to appreciate the rise of "postanalog" capitalism that they have been labeled "Internots." The business community certainly has its share of skeptics who think that "Netizenship" is nothing more than media hype.

But if you're tempted to agree with these skeptics, you should consider the mounting evidence of a paradigm shift. We've hinted at some of this evidence in the Net use statistics. We'll be giving you more, in the form of stories, throughout this book. Are there challenges yet to be met before "connectivity" is complete? Absolutely. But if you think that the Internet explosion is a mere passing fancy, if you think that we can ever go back to a predigital economy, your logical compatriots are the "realists" who snickered at the Wright brothers.

Because the Net, whether you like it or not, has taken off.

The marketing implications are revolutionary. With the rise of E-business, successful business people are obliged to adapt their practices to an electronic, distributed, real-time model. They are forced to think about customers in entirely new ways, to alter their production, marketing, and delivery scenarios, and to adopt new strategies for ensuring customer satisfaction. Some will succeed at this challenge, and many will fail. But no one—not even the "Internots"—will be unaffected by the change.

All of us in business have a wild ride ahead of us, as the old rules of commerce are rewritten and new ones are forged. It will be a frightening ride in some ways, but an exciting one, and we urge you to take it for what it is—an unparalleled opportunity. "Going digital" isn't a hurdle for you to overcome; it is a once-in-a-millennium chance to seize the economic high ground. *Cyber Rules* is designed to help you accomplish that.

Part I

The First Five Years

Chapter 1

The Virtual Marketplace

The Internet and its graphical representation, the World Wide Web, have fired the collective imagination of the business community. So they should. They signal the start of an economic revolution that is destined to transform business from top to bottom. But where will the revolution take us? When it comes to the specifics of the change, even visionaries are only guessing.

This is always true during technological transformations. However brilliant a technology, its social effects are only felt when a critical mass of people adopt it. Before that uptake, the world's most powerful tool is only a gadget. A case in point is ATM banking. Today automated teller machines are more numerous than banks themselves. You can find them on street corners and in supermarkets and airports worldwide. They have turned banking from a business based on "banker's hours" into one where the customer can access money, on a twenty-four/seven basis, almost anywhere in the world. They have become central, indeed indispensable, to today's banking model. If banks had to replace all their ATMs with trained tellers and security people, they would go broke.

Yet the adoption of this automated system was not automatic. Even though ATMs promised shorter lines, fewer errors, and more private transactions, at first people avoided them in droves. They distrusted the machines because they depersonalized the banking experience. In addition, they were slow, they functioned only during limited hours, and they were hard to find. It took the maturing of the underlying technology before ATMs became more reliable—and nearly ubiquitous. Only when that happened did customers begin to understand that they could receive superior service at a reasonable cost by using them.

Today it's hard to imagine a banking system that doesn't use ATMs. Yet the adoption of this technology was not immediate. Similarly, today's E-business on the Internet—distrusted by many, often slow and inefficient—may actually bear little resemblance to its "matured" counterpart. All social revolutions take us in unanticipated directions. Because of that, saying where the Net will be five or ten years from now is a matter of informed speculation.

We don't mind speculating—we'll do some of it in later chapters—but business decisions should be based on what is visible rather than on exotic expectations. So we'll start by describing what is already happening. We'll show you how companies are already profiting handsomely on the Internet, and how their success reveals an Internet that is in many ways different from what early analysts thought it would be.

The Rise of the Virtual Market

The precipitous growth of Internet-enabled business has been most startling, perhaps, at companies that were communications leaders even before the Net surfaced. Among these is the telecommunications giant MCI, which recently merged with another global leader to become MCI-Worldcom. Mike Betzer, one of the expanded company's vice-presidents of information technology, has seen a dramatic change in Internet awareness—and spending—in just the past two years:

> If you looked two years ago at the amount of money we were spending on business-to-business Internet operations, you'd find just scattered skunk groups, people basically in an experimental mode, still on the cusp of development. If you look at our capital structure this year, we will spend more money on the Internet—on Internet systems, customer enablement, and products—than on any other piece of our corporate technology. That's hundreds of millions of dollars. When you realize how quickly the technology is maturing, you know that companies like ours are going to continue to be doing this and that this thing will scale rapidly. There doesn't seem to be anything impeding the growth of Internet business, in fact, except changing the way some of us think. The technology itself is incredibly powerful.

John White, the former chief information officer for Houston-based Compaq, agrees. A computer industry veteran, John was there at the very beginning of the Internet, when it was still in its initial incarnation as the military-based ARPANET. As a Texas Instruments engineer, he was involved in developing an internal packet-switching network as well as a collaborative internal reporting mechanism that, he recalls, was "based on the same premises as the World Wide Web." In John's estimation, the implications of the Internet are unparalleled in the history of communications technology:

> The Internet is going to be the most ubiquitous, cost-effective, and timely mechanism for exchanging information in human history. Coupled with other forms of access, it's already making possible things that were not even conceivable with prior technologies. The telephone and television have also been huge productivity tools to conduct all manner of business, but the Internet outstrips them in enabling us to exchange information collaboratively, visually, and audibly. And the fact that it is so ubiquitous and allows anybody to get access to any form of information makes it probably the most compelling technology that we've ever encountered. Whether it's reading books or selling a product or understanding what's happening in the sports world or stock market, it offers us all a uniquely exciting potential.

What is that potential? As John's invocation of ubiquity implies, it's essentially that the Internet has the ability to connect not just every customer to every business, but *every person on the planet to every other person*. Given that promise, the Internet's most exuberant champions see it as a digital wand that can transform both history and human nature. Because it is global and virtual, they say, it will penetrate national boundaries, dissolve cultural biases, and leap political roadblocks. Being virtual, it will bring information even to those who are forbidden to see it, changing distant corners of the Earth forever by bringing all peoples into a direct connection with the human family.

According to the rhetoric that *Upside* writer Cliff Barney has called "Rapture of the Net," the "mystical network becomes a general-purpose solution for social and cultural problems, a gateway to paradise. We're going to fix the schools, reinvent government, link the world in an orgy of mass communication—and get rich in the process."

This sounds like Hamlet's "consummation most devoutly to be wished," but at this point it's still in the wishing stage—and likely to remain there. What is *not* in the wishing stage is Barney's afterthought—the getting rich part of the mystical equation. There are plenty of companies that are on their way to getting rich in E-business. They are succeeding because of the peculiar suitability of the Internet to streamlining and customizing the buy-sell process.

The rise of E-business has implications for both sides of that process. For those on the "buy" side, Internet technology opens the door to a virtually infinite marketplace. Since distance is irrelevant on the Net, and since contact with potential suppliers can be accomplished instantly, Web-enabled consumers have the world as their shopping place. In that place, they enjoy a *selection* that dwarfs anything hitherto imagined by even the largest supermalls; and a virtual *mobility*, in terms of comparison shopping, that is impossible in the physical world of showrooms and parking lots. For consumers, this is the most obvious advantage of online commerce. It has a radically expansive effect on their capacity to purchase wisely.

That effect is also very *democratizing*. In traditional shopping, where location is a key consideration, the cost of maintaining physical markets makes it difficult for many merchants to carry anything but the most popular items. As a result, many specialized or gourmet goods can only be sold in metropolitan outlets, where there is a concentration of people with high incomes. The demand for *foie gras* is therefore small, making it available only within certain geographical niches. The Internet, however, is capable of offering such low-volume items to a worldwide market because it provides a central sales point, floating inventory, and infinite "connectedness."

Because Web-enabled consumers know this, they are more sophisticated, more demanding, and more empowered than any previous buying population. This empowerment impacts directly on how businesses position themselves—how they *must* position themselves, to survive online. Already corporate leaders in the E-business space have reengineered their internal operating structures to achieve small inventories, just-in-time manufacturing processes, automatic configuration of products to customers' needs, automatic billing, and electronic collection. These are essential features in the emerging E-business model, and they are helping even traditional firms to reinvent themselves.

The advantages to the consumer are obvious enough, but the rise of the virtual market also benefits businesses, although not necessarily in the ways that were originally imagined.

First of all, the automation of business processes and their integration with the Net provide enormous increases in *operating efficiency*. With the low overhead, elimination of paper documentation, and compressed ordering and delivery processes made possible by the Web, businesses are able to appreciate not just economies of scale but what mass customization expert Joe Pine II calls "economies of scope," or the ability to produce greater variety at lower cost.

Second, the economies of the Web are reshaping the *middleman* function. By facilitating direct connections between manufacturers or service providers and end users, the Internet helps to separate mere "transferring" intermediaries from those who add actual value to the buy-sell process. There are significant implications in this move for the economy's macrostructure, and opportunities, as you'll see, for resellers and commerce brokers.

Finally, thanks to distributed and coordinated automation, the boundaries between companies themselves are beginning to blur, accelerating the past decade's trend toward strategic partnerships and creating electronic "marriages" and virtual enterprises. All of these moves in the direction of greater virtuality have made participating firms more responsive and more precise—exactly what they must be to compete in the new "marketspace."

Three Misperceptions

In assessing where the Internet and business will be going, it's just as important to understand where they probably won't be going. As we enter the second generation of the World Wide Web, it is becoming clear that some of the early visions of the new medium's future were little more than technological pipe dreams. Many of those who bet on those dreams have already lost out, leaving the rest of us the opportunity to learn from their mistakes.

Perhaps the first and most oddly persistent of those mistakes was the highway analogy itself. In the early 1990s, when "Netspeak" was the new jargon and the "water cooler effect" was about to transform a military data-exchange system into a popular plaything, the Internet was universally described as an "information superhighway." Every article published in the popular magazines, every hopeful politician's speech, and every starry-eyed educator's vision of the future reinforced the associations that the concept of a physical highway brings to our minds. It suggested the ideas of speed, congestion, on-ramps and exits, and constant, often chaotic, motion.

It also suggested the idea of a "sightseeing" experience—a digital landscape pulsing with electronic billboards that we could not help but look at as we whizzed by. It was this notion of unavoidable billboards that created faith in the Net as an advertising medium. And this faith, unlike the highway metaphor, has proved durable. It has been transferred, you might say, from one spectator metaphor to another: The preferred metaphor, since about 1994, has been not highway driving but channel surfing.

Pipe Dream 1: "It's a television." This is an understandable image, because the Web is highly visual, or graphical. But in spite of the "screen" similarity, a PC is not a television. Television broadcasts a single signal to a waiting audience of millions, and all who are tuned to the same channel share an identical viewing experience. You can decide to surf from channel 4 to channel 57, but even if you have a thousand channels, the information that is coming to you over each one is selected for you at a relatively small number of discrete broadcasting points, and you have no control (except the illusory one of surfing) over what you see.

That isn't at all what happens when you use the Web. The defining characteristic of the Internet as a network is that it has

no central control, no hub, no collection of command centers vying with one another for your attention. When you use the Web,
you determine the mix of what streams in, and that mix may come
from a thousand discrete transmission points, infinitely config-
urable by the individual user and never replicated exactly by any
other viewer. In addition, nobody owns the Web. So what you get
is what you click on, right here and now. It's largely out of the
control of corporate entities.

Unless they actually hit the OFF button, television watchers remain a captive audience—to somebody's message, if not yours;
Web users have a million chances a minute to click elsewhere.
We'll speak more about "clickitis" in the following chapter. Advertisers who consider it an annoyance are missing the point, because idiosyncratic "programming" is the *way* of the Web. This
explains why the Net's advertising potential was initially over-
rated, and why ad executives today are beginning to fear its limitations. A group of them, meeting at a 1998 roundtable, stressed
the uncertainty of online demographics and Web site ratings and
mused that the medium, at best, "has a long way to go before it
can legitimately compete for dollars spent on television or print."

In truth, the Web is less like your television than like another
existing worldwide network—the telephone. With the telephone
network, you dial a number, connect, exchange data (usually in
the form of a conversation), and then hang up. That is exactly
what the "freedom of the Web" lets you do, too. And because of
that freedom, it's a far more challenging medium than mere TV.

When you enter a URL (universal resource locator) address for
a Web site you want to visit, or when you click on an existing hyperlink, the Web server, acting much like a telephone answering
machine, responds to your request by downloading to your

browser a stream of characters that define a Web page; then it breaks the connection. You view the information and if you want more, you put in *another* call to the Web site that returns another prerecorded message, and again it breaks the connection. If the Web page displays data-entry fields, you can send your own message in the form of your name, address, and areas of product interest, and then *you* break the connection. Of course, the information retrieval and branching capabilities provided by search engines and hyperlinks make the Web far quicker and more sophisticated than an answering machine, but the two technologies have still evolved from the same model. Looked at without the hype, the World Wide Web is nothing more than a vast collection of answering machines, each of which sends you graphics and text messages instead of voice recordings.

All of this doesn't mean that advertising and the Web don't mix. They do, but in a unique way. The early idea that you could reap profits by advertising on your Web site turns out to have confused cause and effect. If you wanted to advertise on a worldwide network of answering machines, where would you do it? Not on your corporate answering machine, because you would first need to get your potential customers to call it, just to hear your message. And how would they get the number? Why, from advertising, of course! But advertising in the traditional venues of high traffic flow: print, radio, and (yes) television. You might also throw up a sign on "hot" Internet sites (like the Yahoo! home page), through online services with heavy traffic (like AOL), and through special software applications that push ads to millions of computer desktops.

When customers finally connect, *then* you can do marketing on your Web site, because marketing works best one-on-one. The moral you can draw from this is—in retrospect—a painfully obvious one: If you want to direct traffic to your site, you don't do it *on* the site. Better to turn your answering machine off and advertise in the newspaper.

Pipe Dream 2: "It's a retailer's paradise." A second misperception about the commercial potential of the Net was that it was going to be a retailer's paradise. Businesspeople who anticipated this scenario saw the Web not as "couch potato heaven" but as an "electronic shopping mall." The idea was that, digitized on your home PC screen, the virtual marketplace would offer irresistible "one-stop shopping." Customers would pay an entry fee to enter the mall, and they would do all their shopping in the comfort of their homes.

There are some impressive success stories in online retailing, but in general they are *niche* successes. Analyses show that current electronic malls are attracting lots of computer-literate tire kickers but a disappointing number of serious buyers. In addition, to reach the tens of millions of shoppers who currently aren't even using a computer, electronic malls need to provide a unique advantage to their shopping alternatives, and so far they haven't found a way to do that.

Electronic malls do offer features that conventional shopping cannot. For example, computers and online databases can enable the shopper to "visit" all the stores at once. If the mall provides a large enough variety of electronic stores in its mall, it allows real-time comparative shopping, something that a conventional mall could never supply. Unfortunately, though, given the lack of universal standards for product descriptions, electronic malls only replicate—with a slight increase in speed—the current way we shop. You walk (or click) for hours from one storefront to another and then return to the first store you visited to make a final selection.

The bottom line? Companies that have tried to replicate online the variety and discount possibilities of brick-and-mortar malls have, by and large, been disappointed in their returns. One of the most famous examples, IBM's World Avenue, flopped dramatically. The same fate was visited on Internet Shopping Network, the Web-based version of television's Home Shopping Network.

Retail in general has been less successful than is commonly supposed. Given the oceans of ink that have been devoted to spectacular triumphs like Amazon.com, CDNow, and Dell, this may sound surprising. But it's true. The print splash aside, the bulk of money now being made on the Internet—something on the order of 80 percent—is being made in business-to-business sales, through Web sites that aren't even open to the general public. *Barron's* anticipates that this mix will prevail for some time. They expect retail sales to hit $7 billion by the end of the century—and business-to-business trade to reach $22 billion.

We are seeing a very rapid growth of business-to-business selling, for example, among manufacturers who sell primarily to resellers, third parties, and large corporate buyers. By shifting this type of selling to the Web, where it lends itself very well to being automated, companies are experiencing major savings in time, resources, and sales and marketing overhead, and E-business is quickly growing beyond Web catalog stores.

Cisco is now selling about $2 billion of product quarterly over its Web site through automated business-to-business selling. NEC is automating over $17 billion of supplier business through online procurement. The Charles Schwab Corporation does $2 billion in online securities trades every week. And more and more companies are building completely automated infrastructures. It will only be a matter of time before this type of selling, now highly proprietary, becomes able to support more broad-based business-to-business selling.

What is the role of retail in the Internet future? E-business is all about efficiencies—the efficiencies of greater convenience, lower costs, and added value. With the rapid growth of virtual companies, the value provided by retailers could diminish and it will become profitable for manufacturers to enter the direct-sales business themselves, especially if they can buy powerful, prepackaged E-business tools. In this equation, a normal product retailer becomes a middleman, and as we've mentioned, an efficient electronic market could eliminate many middlemen.

An efficient electronic market in consumer goods could therefore have substantial impact on society. It could eliminate many retail stores in favor of electronic vendors who can locate in areas with low fixed costs, because location is irrelevant on the Internet. This could have massive consequences for countless communities, especially those that have built downtowns or peripheral malls around retail shopping. It could also dramatically impact the manpower mix. We've already seen this happen, and it's going to continue. Companies in the virtual marketplace, rather than hiring clerks with "people skills," show a preference for what the dean of management experts, Peter Drucker, calls "knowledge workers"—people who can enter information quickly into databases, and who can integrate E-business software into existing online systems.

Retail trade will doubtless evolve as marketers come to understand better how to work the Net, and as the small-business sector in particular comes online; as of now, only about a third of that productive sector is wired. But for the immediate generation of Netrepreneurs, including managers and investors, the big Net money is still in nonpublic transactions.

Pipe Dream 3: "We'll wake up rich tomorrow." A final misperception has to do with inevitability. In the early days of the Net, it was widely thought that the natural logic, the trajectory, of the technology itself was a kind of transpersonal force that would ensure quick riches to anyone who was wise enough to put it in place. You might suppose that any savvy businessperson would dismiss this particular pipe dream out of hand, yet the experience of many suggests that it's still going strong. "Companies think millions of dollars will start rolling in a few days after they put up an electronic-commerce application," says Gene McMahon, president of New York reseller BeOnTheNet. "If the process was that easy, I would be sitting on a boat in the Bahamas and sipping martinis."

The fact is that no technology—not even the Internet—has its own trajectory. Like a hammer or an automobile, the Net is a tool that can be wisely or foolishly deployed. It will not drive itself, or drive your stock up, any more than a hammer by itself will build you a dream house. This is pretty elementary stuff, but it's often forgotten, especially by pundits who count the fortunes in Silicon Valley and conclude, "Well, if I had that technology, I'd be successful too."

Consoling, perhaps, but dead wrong. The fact is that the world of E-business is a wide-open field, where access to the technology is only step one. The key to success in this space, as in business in general, is to exceed your customers' expectations—and then do it again. That's a whole lot more challenging than plug-ging in to a server.

The challenge is long term too. We'll emphasize this lesson throughout the book. If you're thinking of entering E-business, expect things to move fast. But do not expect instant profits. You may well wake up rich by utilizing the Internet effectively. But the chances are pretty good that it won't be tomorrow.

What URL Really Means

One lesson of the last few years is that the Web loves a risk taker, even (or maybe especially) one who is willing to break the rules. A second lesson, just as important though less obvious, is that the name of the game, right now, is not revenue but exposure. This is true whether you're building a business that is exclusively virtual, or whether, like literally thousands of established businesses, you are hoping that the Net will supplement your existing operations. In either case, the lesson is to *build a name first.*

If you don't remember anything else about the Web's first five years, remember this: You cannot start too early to build name recognition. Many Internet experts say that the battles for name recognition will be won and lost over the *next three years,* because the greatest growth in the user base will occur during this time as more and more customers turn to online buying. Many sites are therefore scrambling to build their brand names before these new electronic buyers' habits are set.

Those who are successful will reap the rewards of new cus-tomer acquisition and the establishment of market leadership po-sitions in narrow segments of the online market. The online stock brokerage AmeriTrade found that out recently, when it spent $25 million in advertising in a single quarter to promote its new $8 per trade price. Heavy investment, yes. But the payback was an immediate gain of 51,000 new customers in three months, and a more powerful market presence that helped them compete against other online brokers.

By being too cautious here, you may count yourself out. That is true even if you have a recognized brand name in a traditional business. If you don't solidify your name recognition in this wide-open new space, there is no guarantee that playing catch-up later will enable you to displace the smart online leader.

Joe Walowski, whose Red Wagon start-up is fighting it out in the tough world of online grocery delivery, has it right: "Forget about revenue; right now it's a market-share war. You've got to stake out your niche, figure out what the boundaries are for your particular business, and then you gotta nail it. You gotta be the winner in that market."

That is as true in computer chips as in potato chips. Listen to Eric Schmidt, chairman and CEO of Novell. In a 1997 speech, he alluded to the urgency of getting seen before you get rich. Be everywhere first, he said, then think about profit. "You have to get the revenue later; ubiquity first, revenue later. That's what URL stands for."

It's a comment that is as accurate as it is clever. Eric expanded on it in a recent conversation, as he reflected on the often noted fact that the stock valuations of many Internet companies seemed wildly disproportionate to their P&L profiles.

Historically, people get confused over stock market valuations and business valuations. The stock values use various proxies for forward profitability, and in this emerging market, what has been clear for three or four years is that the stock market will allow you to lose an almost infinite amount of money as long as you can convince them that you're gaining in some other metric that they care about. In Internet businesses, that metric is either subscribers, users, or eyeballs. So the closer to ubiquitous users you are, the better your valuation. That's why Netscape, to take just one famous early example, was valued so highly at first. Everybody believed that they had a very, very large and profound user base.

Of course, history now shows that that kind of user base isn't necessarily permanent, and that's interesting in itself. But it doesn't change the principle. If you want to get backing or stock support for an Internet venture, it's really easy. You just get up and announce, "The biggest thing in the world is about to happen." Explain how it's going to happen, and then say, "And by the way, we're going to get 80 percent market share." You start out by promoting that vision, not this quarter's revenues.

Of course, you can only play this game so many times in so many ways. If I announced that I was going to try to gain market share in nuclear reactors, you wouldn't give me money for that because while it's a very large market, in terms of potential dollars, it's not a market that's strategic or growing or profitable. So it comes back to this old idea about banking on a vision. You've got to present a story that people believe.

We've seen this since the advent of the Internet, and the market has still not stopped doing it. It's still willing to grant Amazon.com time to expand—whatever their balance sheets say—as long as it's expanding in a unit or market share way.

That's another way of saying ubiquity. Market share first, revenue later.

As counterintuitive as it may be to P&L–driven marketers, business leaders are gradually getting this message. A recent survey of business executives performed by an independent research group on behalf of Spiral Media, Inc., showed that the most significant value of a Web site was not increased sales revenues, but improved customer service and increased company recognition. Over 70 percent of them mentioned brand recognition and better customer relations, while only 55 percent expected better retail sales.

For the time being, at least, that's the right approach. In the virtually infinite market of online business, the future belongs to those who market infinitely.

Chapter 2

Problems and Prospects

What are the major difficulties facing E-business?

As of now, they may be broken down into two categories. Ask anyone involved in doing business on the Internet what he sees as the chief impediments to online expansion, and whatever you hear is likely to contain these words: "data access" and "security." This chapter addresses these two concerns.

The Problem with Data

For all practical purposes, online data is infinite. Unfortunately, it wanders in cyberspace without any sense of consistent organization. On one Web page, a product description might be in one place. On another Web page, the same or a similar description might be in a totally different place. Data on the Web is truly chaotic. There are no standards for how it should be categorized or displayed, and this severely limits the ability of marketers and customers to find the relevant business information that they need.

We address this problem by employing search engines—Infoseek, Yahoo!, Excite—to help sort through the glut. Different search engines work in different ways, but one common method used is to scan the WWW for new Web pages, strip the full text from these pages, store this in large fast-retrieval databases, and then index the entries based on keywords. To locate information from these databases, you enter keywords that reflect the subject you are searching for, and the engines use them to deliver various "hits," order ranked by the quality of the matches found.

It sounds great, and it's certainly impressive, as anyone will tell you who has ever typed in a keyword like "peanuts" and gotten 10,000 responses. But that's exactly the problem. Search engines tend to return any and all information that matches simple patterns, with the hits having no context, meaning, or structure. To make matters worse, search engines only scratch the surface of the existing Web. According to a *Wall Street Journal* report, the most comprehensive of them, HotBot, indexes 34 percent of today's Web pages; the least comprehensive, Lycos, sifts through only 3 percent. It's like they're attempting to dig through Mount Everest with a teaspoon. And the mountain itself is growing.

How can we base a future of E-business on the data-access and data-representation methodologies of today's WWW? At the very least, any E-business application must be able to find simple information about a product such as its name, its description, and its price. Yet data organization today is so wildly disorganized that it presents the highest possible technical challenge simply to define search strategies and technologies that compensate for the lack of universal representation standards.

One ray of hope is in an emerging standard known as extensible markup language, or XML, which is designed specifically to make Web-based data more usable. With XML, you should be able to build data-driven Web programs that allow the definition of structured data for each Web site. An XML "tag" defines the meaning of data, not its appearance. For example, one tag might be called "product name" and another might be "price." By being able to extract this meaningful information from a Web site, we have the ability to begin to support a much enhanced version of E-business on the Internet.

It is in the operation of Web search engines that XML may have the most dramatic effect. The consistent use of XML—or some other standard—on all Web sites will provide the opportunity for universal "intelligent searching." A far easier and more long-lasting solution for the messy data problem is elegant in its simplicity: Organize the data on the Web page itself. Define simple standards for online sellers. Agree on how to represent products, and how and where to represent their prices, so that an automatic program, without human intervention, can access a Web page, gain useful information from it, and make some simple but well-informed buying decisions. We're not talking about futuristic software here but about software programs that do what standard financial programs do right now: find data in a known format from a known source, operate on it, and create results.

E-business must eventually be supported by a worldwide effort to organize information on the Internet. This is coming. It has to, because without such advances in data representation and accessibility, E-business will be severely constrained. By centralizing the Web's mounting data for automatic access, we lay the foundation for applications to use this data efficiently and offer capabilities that we have never before experienced.

But data glut, exacerbated by the lack of organizational standards, represents only one half of the data-access problem. The other half concerns the computer industry's favorite whipping boy: inadequate bandwidth. The lack of adequate bandwidth—that is, the capacity of the Internet to carry and deliver information to your desktop—is a constant source of irritation for many users. It's a problem that everybody moans about, but often without recognizing that there are actually two different areas in which the information "pipe" can become congested: on the network itself and at the connection to your telephone-dependent modem.

The Net Proper

We should say "nets," because in spite of the implication of unity in its name, *the* Internet is not a single network. It is a combination of thousands of different private networks that are joined at certain exchange points throughout the world. At these exchange points, high-speed digital switches transfer data traffic from one network to another. This is why you're able to send e-mail to someone anywhere in the world, as long as he is connected at some point with one of the carriers of major Internet traffic.

America Online, for example, is a large private network connecting millions of subscribers. Not only can an AOL user send e-mail to someone with an Internet address, but Internet users can also address their e-mail to any individual AOL user. Cerfnet, another major Internet service provider (ISP), uses five major connection points in the continental United States, connecting to seventeen other networks through a San Jose, California, exchange point affectionately called MAE-West (Metropolitan Access Exchange-West) and to twenty-six others through an equivalent exchange point in New York (MAE-East). It also has dedicated high-speed data lines allowing Cerfnet traffic to be sent across the breadth of the country, providing better service for its customers than many smaller ISPs that don't have this national data-delivery capability.

You've probably heard about the "backbone" of the Internet. Here, too, the singular is a misnomer, for there are actually a number of major international providers—MCI-Worldcom and UUNET are among the leaders—which comprise the central skeleton of this vast system. Even though they are privately owned, these individual backbones provide common data-transport service through the interconnection points with other networks.

Since every Internet message, or "packet," contains the address where it will ultimately be sent, individual network routers along the way can read this address, determine the most efficient path to the destination, and then send that packet on the next step of its electronic journey. But because each router can make a new path decision, you cannot predetermine the exact path that an individual packet will take on its journey through the Internet.

This is one of the Internet's most important features—a design implanted in the early military-funded phase of the system that enables it to continue functioning even if part of it is incapacitated by sabotage. Routers can also detect nodes that are not operating properly and send packets around them, even if the trouble is only a temporary traffic overload. This load-balancing feature is intended to smooth out the flow of data, guaranteeing optimal bandwidth for everyone connected.

The system works fine, except in those situations when a temporarily high level of usage on the Internet, or on your subnetwork piece of it, has a "spike" effect on the operation of the system—and on the bandwidth that comes through as available to you. This isn't totally haphazard. Such overload slowdowns occur regularly at peak usage periods (usually from 11 A.M. to 2 P.M. local time). At those times, as the network becomes saturated, a high proportion of new packets introduced onto the network may be lost, and will have to be retransmitted. This retransmission introduces time delays.

In addition, individual Internet components sometimes go down, or lines are cut, which affect areas beyond a local market. One famous regional crash occurred on July 16, 1997, when a faulty voltage breaker at San Jose's MAE-West cut off Internet traffic at that central location, forcing multiple ISPs to route their data to alternate switchpoints. Smaller ISPs that didn't have such alternatives were removed from the global Internet completely. When MAE-West became unavailable, other connect points had to take the traffic normally shared among many switches, and the Internet quickly became unusable for the remaining ISPs and their customers. Glitches like this, rare as they are, show us the potential seriousness of bandwidth congestion, and because of this, ISPs and telephone companies are feverishly developing technologies to keep ahead of demand.

Many of the bandwidth problems lie with the ISPs themselves, some of which have not been keeping up with available technology. Having slow routers and few interconnection points to backbone providers will eventually mean poor service to customers, occasionally introducing ripple effects on connected networks. And while many network service providers are upgrading their own network infrastructures, this can be expensive and slow. In the meantime, demand for bandwidth is increasing daily.

There are also new uses of the WWW that threaten to clog the arteries of the Internet. The popular use of so-called "push technology," where selective data is broadcast (or more properly *narrow-cast*) to millions of home computers, promises to raise significantly the average level of Internet traffic. In addition, the increasing availability of advanced multimedia computers in the home, with their ability to display compressed video at high-frame rates, is going to spur the demand to bring this capability into the home, and this will put further strains on the network's capabilities.

Plain Old Telephone Slowness

The backbone of the Internet is digital, and it is increasingly made up of fiber-optic links providing large bandwidths. Local Internet service providers are rapidly upgrading their equipment to fiber optics as well, and within a few years they will be capable of offering subscribers wider bandwidth on demand. But, as has been often reported, the last mile of the globally connected Internet, the one that takes data into the home and connects the retail consumer, is the weakest link in the chain. This last step uses the plain old telephone service (POTS), which runs on copper wire, to connect home computers to the Net at speeds far slower than any other data link in the world.

If you connect through a modem, you can receive data only as fast as your modem can deliver it, and typical home modems to-day provide rates of only 28.8Kbps (thousand bits per second) to 56Kbps. This means that even the fastest modem available is thirty times slower than a basic T1 line—the current standard for providing commercial Internet access. So even if your Internet service provider can carry data at much faster speeds than that, you are not now in a position to take advantage of it. In a sense, the modem is a relic, a technological "kludge" that attempts to span the gap between the old analog world of the past and the new digital world of the future. It is reaching for the speed and clarity of a bit-and-byte universe but trying to do this, anachro-nistically, by utilizing the existing twisted copper wire connec-tions in the most brute force manner possible, taking up the complete theoretical communication capacity of those wires by sending analog data instead of digital.

Most experts predict that, despite the increasing availability of faster connections to the Internet, the modem may remain the In-ternet link for the majority of home users for some time. Because of this, and because most retail buying will take place from home computers, this bandwidth limitation directly affects the growth and evolution of retail E-business. Unless a dramatic shift in In-ternet-to-home connection technology takes place, retail shop-ping on the Internet will not come into its own for at least five years.

That shift is coming, though, inevitably. In the near future, data links to homes and businesses will be made universally through optical fibers capable of carrying an almost infinite data load, as well as direct satellite access, making high-speed remote Internet access a reality. It will happen. Given the logic of the Net, there's no alternative.

Bandwidth Improvements

Increased demands on the Internet's infrastructure will make our online experience worse before it gets better. But it *will* get better. Already, at the network level, current router technology from such vendors as Cisco Systems, Inc.; Bay Networks, Inc.; and 3Com allows the delivery of up to 500,000 packets per second. Now in design and development are the next generation of routers that will be able to deliver as much as 30 million packets per second, a sixtyfold increase in throughput.

We are also seeing improvements at the server level. In the past, ISPs used T1 lines (1.5Mbps) to deliver an Internet connection into corporate networks, with T3 lines (45Mbps) serving as their national backbones. Today technology is leapfrogging these older technologies, with many companies now using optical cables to transmit over OC-3 links (155Mbps). UUNET just completed a major upgrade to its cross-country backbone connections to OC-12 (622Mbps) capacity. PSINet, another major provider, has negotiated for the rights to use a new Internet backbone that uses OC-48 technology, operating at 2.4 billion bps, fifty times faster than a T3 line. This is an encouraging trend, promising to provide whatever bandwidth tomorrow's Internet applications will require.

Massachusetts Institute of Technology media guru Nicholas Negroponte extols the carrying capacity of fiber optics as virtually infinite. "We literally do not know how many bits per second we can send down a fiber," he writes. "Recent research results indicate that we are close to being able to deliver 1,000 billion bits per second. This means that a fiber the size of a human hair can deliver every issue ever made of *The Wall Street Journal* in less than one second. . . . And, mind you, I am talking of a single fiber, so if you want more, you just make more. It is, after all, just sand."

For home users—including the vast retail customer base—there is also some hope on the horizon. Cable modems are becoming more and more popular, as cable companies begin to see the business value they have through owning existing customer data connections and as online businesses in general begin to appreciate their speed. That speed is a considerable improvement over current modems. For example, a file that would take eight minutes to download over a standard 28.8K modem would take only *eight seconds* through a cable modem.

Finally, there is lower-orbiting satellite (LEO) technology. Several companies are now rolling out LEOs that orbit just a few hundred miles overhead, eliminating the lag-time of geosynchronous satellites. Teledesic, a new company funded by Greg McCaw (of McCaw Cellular) and Bill Gates of Microsoft, promises true "Internet in the sky" service. It will allow any remote user to establish a 2Mbps connection from anywhere on the earth, at rates comparable to today's connect fees. This is the clear beginning of a new age of high-speed, universal, wireless data communications that will cover the planet, and that will eventually provide more bandwidth capacity than we have people or data to fill.

Novell's chairman and CEO, Eric Schmidt, echoed this optimism in a recent conversation, as he anticipated imminent solutions to the "last mile" problem:

As a general rule, the Internet is somewhere between tripling and quadrupling every year, depending on what numbers you use. And the underlying backbone of the Internet, now that all that fiber-optic capacity got turned on, has almost infinite bandwidth compared to its use. If you can get yourself connected to the backbone, for all practical purposes you have essentially no access problems.

But—and it's a but with important implications—you're still limited by something that's not related to bandwidth. The Internet industry is now suffering the same problem that the telephone company has suffered for years, which is the last mile problem, the slow modem connection. The remaining question is: How do I get a megabyte, a continuous persistent megabyte, available to every person, every supplier or partner, every customer?

This world of 33.6 and 128K modems and so forth is really a transitional period. The next logical step is to cable modems, because they're able to deliver at the megabyte capacity. So can the cellular radio technologies, which unlike dial-up connections are always on. In other words, the connection is always there.

So at this stage, the model that you want to start thinking about is not the bandwidth problem—that's essentially fixed—but what happens to electronic commerce when everyone is connected to the Net with a device that gives them a continuous megabyte. When every home and every office has access to that. That's a whole new level, a whole new range of possibilities.

In a speech to industry leaders a couple of years ago, Eric quoted a friend, former FCC chairman Reed Hundt, describing his particular vision of Internet heaven. "What we need," said Hundt, "is a high-speed, congestion-free, always reliable, friction-free, packet-switched, big-bandwidth, data-friendly network that is universally available, competitively priced, and capable of driving our economy to new heights." Eric's wry response? "Makes sense to me."

It makes sense to us, too. And, as Eric rightly pointed out, we're already building it. With the advent of fiber optics and satellite hookups, we are at the forefront of a historical shift in which analog communication walks off into the sunset and is replaced by fully digitized, broad-stream delivery. The potential for E-business is nothing less than phenomenal.

What about the other major concern, security? To answer this question, let's look first at the most personal level.

Privacy: Whose Life Is It, Anyway?

Every time you use a credit card, you create an electronic trace of what you just did. Strung together, these traces comprise a dynamic history of your activities. If you have been using credit cards for many years, you have already surrendered a huge amount of personal information that is sitting on the disk drives of individual businesses, credit bureaus, and government agencies. Your credit card number alone is probably stored on several hundred computer systems around the world.

Our collective privacy used to be protected by the fact that information existed on paper—a medium that is slow to use, often difficult to access, and degradable. In the quick, open, and durable world of the Net, there are few practical limits to what can be done with, or to, databased "private" information, or to how quickly it can be made available to "authorized" parties. So the question of security begins at the personal level.

This fact puts an odd spin on the value of information. From the perspective of efficiency, we want all we can get: instant information at our fingertips, exactly when we want it. But what if it's information about *us*? Do we want that available? To whom, and for what purposes, are we willing to reveal ourselves? More to the point, to whom do we *not* want to reveal ourselves?

Although concerns over "Big Brother" have not completely died out, most people today are less worried about the government's intrusion into our private lives than about our private information being used to our economic disadvantage. We're less concerned about the federal government stealing our identities than we are about having a scam artist use our card number to fly to Cancún. But don't count the government out. The evolving networked infrastructure and digital data repositories may provide an irresistible lure to government bureaucrats who want to know as much about you as possible—solely for "your own good," of course.

One technology that makes it easier for them to do so goes by the friendly name of "cookies." A cookie is an electronic tracking tag that a Web site owner may place on a visitor's browser to make identification of that visitor easier the next time he or she visits. There is some concern about the use of this technology not only by government but by E-business marketers as well. Because cookies can be placed on a browser without the user's knowledge, one *Wired* editor warns that a tug-of-war is developing between advocates of full disclosure and defenders of the status quo. Few observers would go so far as Apple computer executive Allen Olivo in predicting that cookies could be "the death of the Internet," but many agree that they're an invasion of electronic privacy, and this is a perception that the online community is currently wrangling with.

The advent of cookies is only one of the problems. Another is garbage. You've heard the slogan "Garbage In, Garbage Out." It means that computerized records, whether they're secure or insecure, are only as reliable as the human being who created them; that is, the people who input the data in the first place. Since people are fallible, errors are continually creeping in to computer databases. And once an error is "in there," it can be hell to get it out. Or to get people to believe that it *should* be gotten out.

Consider, for example, the story of Bronti Kelly. After suffering an embarrassing, costly, and inexplicable string of job losses, Kelly discovered that his extraordinary bad luck was the result of an error in a computer database. The database was used to run background checks on prospective employees, and every time an employer accessed Kelly's records, the database reported that he had been convicted of burglary, shoplifting, and arson. Not exactly prime employee material.

But the real felon wasn't the physical Kelly. It was his electronic avatar, the "Kelly" who was represented by his credit cards. A thief had filched his wallet, stolen the cards, and assumed his identity in a series of major crimes. That was bad enough, but here was the kicker. The felon had obviously violated the boundaries of E-privacy, but when Kelly tried to access his own files to correct the record, he was told that they were unavailable to him. Hence the ultimate irony, if not the ultimate glitch: An innocent party is "protected" from his own records, while the system is fair game to hackers and cyberthieves.

Kelly finally managed to track down the error, and he sued the background check company, Stores Protective Association, for millions. That in itself should be a cautionary note for E-businesses. And it helps to explain why, amid rising concern about "cybersnoop" intrusiveness, there is a growing interest in creating standards governing privacy on the Internet. It's a consumer-generated initiative to which vendors should pay heed.

One Internet privacy initiative, sponsored by Firefly Network, Inc., Netscape Communications, and Microsoft, is focused on defining a set of standards for controlling how users determine how their personal information is exchanged over the Web. This standard, called the open profiling standard (OPS), provides a framework with built-in privacy safeguards to cover user information exchanged between individuals and E-business sites. If adopted, it will guarantee that in the future, even though there may exist many different bits and bytes of personal information scattered across the span of the Web, you will have the ability to control how that information is shared with others.

With this proposal, this profile information can be stored at a vendor's site, on the buyer's computer, or in a shared, secure online repository that trusted users could have access to. Of course, security then becomes a major issue, because it would take only a single break-in of a central repository of profiles to bring the entire system down. It's an ongoing story to which E-business players should stay tuned.

Cyber Crime

Theft of computerized information has been around since the advent of computers, but before the existence of networks and digital data, criminals were obliged to go physically where the information was kept. No longer. Today, with nothing more than a computer (not necessarily a very powerful one), a data connection to the target (which is more and more being provided by the Internet), and a knowledge of software cracking techniques, a dedicated cyberthief need not leave his or her house.

In fact, he need not even be in the same country. Because the Internet is international in scope, crackers can sit safely behind country borders and mount successful attacks on targets all over the world. And, depending on what country they operate from, they may not even be breaking any local laws! Some notorious examples:

- In May, 1997, a hacker in the San Francisco area tapped into a local ISP, intercepting network data from a dozen online companies selling products on the Internet. He was able to access its contents directly, eventually collecting over 100,000 credit card numbers. He was caught only after he tried to sell the information to an undercover FBI agent for $260,000.

- In September 1997, the U.S. extradited a Russian hacker from Britain, where he had been lured to get him out of Russia. Vladimir Levin was accused of withdrawing more than $10 million from Citibank accounts all over the world. He did this with an old computer through a standard telephone line from his tiny office in St. Petersburg. He was caught only because some of his accomplices were arrested and fingered him.

- The *London Times* reported in June of 1996 that several financial institutions had paid over $400 million to extortionists who threatened to destroy their global financial operations through deliberately placing "logic bombs"—software programs designed to mangle data—on corporate computers.

The truth is that most computer systems of U.S. companies and federal sites are not secure. The Defense Information Systems Agency's internal testing procedures, in fact, successfully crack "secure" Department of Defense computer sites about 65 percent of the time. Given that the DOD reports over 250,000 hacker attacks each year, you have to believe that real break-ins occur with some frequency. If a hacker can penetrate the Pentagon, how secure is your company?

Perhaps the most significant and alarming security trend is the increasing involvement of *governments* in the theft of corporate secrets. The CIA has identified France, China, Russia, Japan, Israel, Cuba, and Iran as the countries most frequently engaged in illegal industrial espionage in the United States. Concern over "friendly" nations such as Israel and France engaging in industrial, economic, and trade espionage against the United States has prompted the passage of a new law (the Industrial Espionage Act of 1996) that provides sanctions against foreign agents who attack U.S. companies. In the first application of this law, General Motors won $100 million in damages against a foreign company that had developed a vehicle based on data stolen from GM.

What does all this activity mean? Exactly how vulnerable are we?

Remember first that *any* computer-based system is vulnerable to attack. As companies move on to the Internet, they become even more vulnerable, because connection to the Net exposes them at more entry points. When you've got a true "virtual" company, operating on a system of electronic linkages, any disruption in any of these linkages, through either a security breach, a system failure, or an electronic attack, might cause at least the temporary failure of that virtual business. Multiply this by a million times and you will get a glimpse of the not-too-distant future: every business in the world connected to every other business, and all of it vulnerable to attack by E-creeps and -crooks.

The U.S. government is not unaware of network security problems, and is looking to solve them. The General Accounting Office, for example, has begun testing the federal financial system for weak links. Using a software program, it deliberately tries to penetrate banks and FedWire, the national network carrying Federal Reserve banking transactions. The GAO is also anticipating physical attacks, such as the "explosion" of electronic bombs that can fry computer circuits. Placing one of these outside the Richmond Federal Reserve, for example, could potentially bring the entire system down, completely paralyzing the Federal Reserve System. Our growing dependence on the Internet is making us ever more vulnerable to attack, and this trend, for the foreseeable future, will not very likely be reversed.

If security technology doesn't keep pace with those who attempt to break it, Net-based commerce will break down at its weakest point. So keeping pace is a matter of E-business survival. How do we do it?

Security Solutions: Protecting the Firewall

The problem of Internet security is, in principle, quite simple. Because you have an Internet connection, you have potentially exposed your previously secure system to the world. The issue is not about having a Web site through which external users access your system. The problem is being connected to the Internet at all. Period. A Net connection is a gateway to the external world, a doorway through which anyone with Internet access can attempt to break into your internal computer system. How do you admit legitimate visitors and keep others out? An initial step is to monitor protocols at your company "firewall."

Protocols and the firewall. The Internet, unlike most internal networks (Intranets), supports many different types of connection protocols, each one regulating the exchange of a particular type of data. For each protocol, there is an associated connection "port" that is established between a company's client and server. One of these, file transfer protocol (FTP), permits the downloading and uploading of file information between different sites. Allowing unrestricted FTP access to *any* machine on your internal system is tantamount to opening up your entire site to the outside.

To prevent this, companies adopt various security measures to create what is commonly known as a protective "firewall." A firewall can be software, hardware, or a combination of the two. Its principal function is to serve as an application-level gateway, allowing safe external connections to internal applications. Software and application connect rules must be defined, and must be unique to a given application. Used correctly, application gateways provide a high level of security and should make it almost impossible for untrusted external users to execute an internal application—such as, for example, your company's accounts receivable software.

Encryption. Unwanted users can also be kept on the far side of your firewall through a coding process known as encryption. If data is sent as unmodified "clear text," it is perilously available to anyone who cares to read it—whether or not you or your customers want him to do so. If you were involved in an online transaction and it was sent in clear text, someone could potentially intercept your name, address, and credit card number, just as the San Francisco hacker recently did. But not if it's in code, and that's why we encrypt.

But encryption, as logical as it sounds, is not without its problems. Among them is the issue of government oversight.

It is the United States government that defines what level of security is legal, and this level is controlled by something quite simple in principle: the size (in bits) of the security key used to encrypt. As of today, the government allows a maximum 40-bit key for export, with a 56-bit length for U.S.–based applications. While it is always a difficult operation to decrypt any encrypted message, the smaller the key the easier it is to break a code, which means that the 40-bit code is more vulnerable than the 56-bit one.

You might reasonably ask: If security is good, isn't better security better? Why wouldn't the government want all of us to have a 56-bit key? The answer is that they don't want the bad guys to get it. To maintain an edge in the war on electronic crime, the FBI wants control over the harder-to-crack code. And they want to dramatically restrict its export. It's the equivalent of prohibiting certain firearms (AK47s, for example) among the potentially criminal citizenry, and it meets exactly the same kind of objection that gun control does: If 56-bit keys are outlawed, only outlaws will have them.

Give us all the better key, say laissez-faire advocates, so we can have as much firewall power as the criminals themselves. The FBI has fought that logic for years, insisting that regulation of encryption is a national necessity. But recent developments may have the government bending. First, the FBI offered to liberalize encryption export standards as long as they could get a copy of the relevant keys. In this "backdoor" accommodation, the idea was that the key would be on file somewhere, available on demand, if needed, to any law-enforcement agency. We need an E-version of the wiretap, said the FBI. All of your telephone communications are secure, except in those cases where there is justification to listen in. The same principle would apply for a digital tap.

Privacy advocates say that the backdoor approach would require a massive new federal program just to support the creation and maintenance of key storage and recovery. This would mean that any individual, organization, or company performing data encryption would have to register its secure key with a key-management service, and many computer professionals consider this to be unworkable.

In March 1998, the FBI bent again, backing off from its "no export" policy and hoping for a negotiated peace with open-market advocates. "Law enforcement is concerned," said bureau lobbyist Barry Smith, "that we have the technical capability under strict legal procedures to gain access to the plain text of criminally related communications or electronically stored data. We're willing to sit down . . . to see if we can meet our goals through good-faith dialogue."

With the outcome still in doubt, encryption is clearly another issue to which all E-business players should stay tuned.

Authentication. In any business transaction, both parties need to offer a guarantee of their identities. Sometimes authentication is as simple as providing a password. In E-business, authentication can be accomplished in a number of ways, including the use of encryption technologies that perform authentication as well as encryption.

Authentication requires, among other things, a digital "signature." The process begins with a mathematical summary called the "hash code," which acts as a compressed representation and unique "fingerprint" of the message. The hash code is then encrypted with the sender's private key attached to the message. When the message is received, the hash code attached to the message is compared to another hash code calculated by the recipient. If the two match, then the recipient knows that the message has indeed come from the sender, that it has not been altered, and that its integrity has not been compromised.

Keys for digital signatures are filed in a public-key directory, made up of individual user "certificates" that serve to verify identities, like a bank's physical signature cards. A trusted certification authority manages and distributes these certificates, in addition to electronic keys.

Access control.

Access control determines who can get access to a local or remote computer system or network, as well as what privileges are granted when he or she logs on. Access to information can be restricted at the document level by access-control lists, which itemize the resources that individual users can access. In addition, access-control mechanisms can be distributed on the network. The mechanisms do not have to reside on the same host as the Web site. This means that administrators can physically operate the access-control services on a separate host, allowing multiple Web sites to make use of the same access-control mechanisms.

Many enterprise systems are now using "smart cards" that complement the existing log on methods. With a reader attached to the client, absolutely secure client/server authorization can take place, guaranteeing that the card is trusted. Stealing the card will of course give the holder an additional opportunity to break in, but the combination of a simple PIN number and the card has proved to be a theoretically unbreakable combination.

From Plastic to Electrons: How to Pay Online

All security issues, and the attendant business risks, come together over the issue of online payment. Much current work in the network security industry focuses on making E-payment both efficient and reliable.

Because of the inherent hackability of the Internet, E-business transactions require far more rigorous security to protect confidentiality of the transactions that occur, and of the transfer of high-value assets. This is a relatively minor issue in business-to-consumer Internet commerce because many security problems are solved by credit cards. Credit cards allow spontaneous transactions without the need for individual buyers and sellers to know and trust one another. For security, card users depend on an intermediary such as an issuing bank or credit card company that qualifies individual card-holders, extends them credit, does credit checks and revokes cards for lack of payment, and constantly detects and manages fraud.

If network security breaks down and an improper transaction takes place, the established credit card infrastructure comes into play and handles the problem, guaranteeing, for example, that merchants will be paid and that, under federal law, users are liable for only fifty dollars of a fraudulent transaction. So while no one wants to open additional doors to credit card fraud, the current Internet system does not introduce any more risk into the payment process than the model that is currently supported by the Plain Old Telephone System.

The same isn't true in business-to-business transactions. Because they can involve large amounts of money and can contain highly sensitive corporate data, they need a better security platform than the ones provided with credit card systems. Yet in the business-to-business model that currently exists, there is no substitute for the credit card on a wide-scale basis. Today, each time a company seeks a new business partner, it must qualify the buyer or seller, check credit, negotiate terms, set up accounts payable and receivable, and incur the costs of order-taking, invoicing, payment, and collection. It can be a pretty expensive process.

Currently, the Internet lacks a standard form of digital money—some kind of fast, easy, and secure way to let consumers buy and sell electronically. Today, many merchants' practices, and many popular Internet-based payment systems, are still based on credit cards. But a rash of high-profile security issues has caused many people to lose faith with credit card encryption as a truly secure line for electronic payment. Hence the emergence of digital cash alternatives.

The exchange of digital cash represents the exchange of electronic tokens. In an electronic token system, tokens can be stored on a user's card or computer and can be exchanged directly between remote transacting parties. This exchange does not require a fixed network infrastructure and can be accomplished through an intermittent network connection or even a handheld device. So there are real advantages here. Nonetheless, electronic cash replacements have had trouble gaining public mind share. In consummating online transactions, most people still depend, despite all of their protestations to the contrary, on their credit cards.

No doubt this has something to do with the perception that electronic money isn't "real" money. To many, electronic cash represents nothing tangible except an electronic number, first in a bank account and then as a set of electrons passed along a wire to a home computer, and then as an arrangement of magnetic domains on a hard disk. When you pay with these electronic analogs, you merely send signals from your computer to another computer, and although your balance is debited, you never handle anything concrete; it's all just numbers. That bothers some people.

It shouldn't, though, because when you come right down to it, credit cards aren't real money, either. Nor, for that matter, is the one-dollar bill that the Treasury Department says you can redeem for Fort Knox gold. *All* money is a conventional marker of value.

It's just that plastic "money" has been around for decades, and the electronic equivalent is still struggling for general recognition.

When we do learn to accept electronic cash, we will find that it has significant advantages over our credit cards. First, it operates much like an ATM. You withdraw a certain amount and carry it with you away from your bank. Because a credit card involves a credit transaction, there are a lot of steps in the process, each contributing unavoidable processing fees. E-cash is carried on your computer instead of in your pocket and transferred by wires, so you don't even have to go outside to make a withdrawal. And because there are no processing fees, you can pay even small amounts without worry.

Each amount of e-cash carries an irrefutable signature from the bank that issued it, a highly secure digital signature. This makes it impossible to counterfeit. Even though each piece of e-cash also carries a unique serial number that only your computer could generate, the bank cannot know what this serial number is and thus can't trace any purchase or payment you make through e-cash back to its source. E-cash is completely anonymous, just like paper bills.

However, should you choose to, or should the government force you to, you can irrefutably prove that a specific payment to a specific party came from you, and only you. For example, if you were the source of an e-cash payment to a black marketer or extortionist, this could be absolutely determined with your cooperation and with data from your computer. So replacing paper and coins with e-cash will make life much more difficult for future criminals.

Secure Electronic Transaction Protocol

In addition to digital cash, there is an emerging standard for Internet credit card transactions called secure electronic transaction (SET). The still struggling protocol, released in the summer of 1997, provides software specifications for the three parties generally involved in an E-business transaction: the cardholder, the merchant, and the acquiring bank. SET stipulates the certification process and certificate formats for each of these parties, as well as the encryption and authentication methodology for financial transactions. Taken together, these elements define a system that is reasonably secure and sufficiently open to allow credit card–based payment to be deployed over the course of the next few years.

There has been important progress with SET, including two very visible SET transactions. On October 5, 1997, VISA International announced that it had completed two SET-compliant transactions in Latin America and in Asia, with banks, financial service providers, and VISA members taking part. Participants in the Latin American SET program used a VISA card to purchase a bottle of wine from a supermarket in Buenos Aires and to purchase a book from an office-supply company in São Paulo. A second SET 1.0–compliant transaction took place in Tokyo, hours after the Latin American project. This project, which utilized "smart cards," involved the cooperation of VISA, Toshiba Corporation, CyberCash, IBM, Netscape, and VeriSign.

In spite of these SET showcases, nobody is saying the bugs have been worked out yet. For full deployment, SET will require that a certificate exist for each consumer credit card to be used on the Internet. That will entail substantial administrative overhead. Processes also need to be in place to account for issues of certificate revocations, loss of PIN numbers, and the possible cancellation of certificates. In addition, although SET describes what will be needed for credit card authorization and purchase, it does not cover online payment through other means, such as e-cash, e-check, debit, and micropayments. These may be increasingly important as E-business grows.

Some observers are suggesting that the day of this innovative protocol has already passed. In the long time (by Internet standards) that it has taken to roll SET out, consumers have become increasingly comfortable with using their plastic on the Net. Virtual Vineyards' marketing director Cyndy Ainsworth cites a "dramatic increase" in the number of card-using customers, and a survey of Internet users found that, although online shoppers *say* they're still concerned about Net security, nearly 60 percent of them have used a credit card online anyway. Will SET become a solution in search of a problem?

The View from Compaq

Let's tie up this chapter with some comments from an industry colleague who has been observing the Net's problems and prospects from its very beginnings. John White is the former chief information officer of the Houston-based computer giant Compaq, and he has been working in this space since the infant medium was still called ARPANET. Thinking about the dangers of our drowning in unsortable data, John has this to say about the access problem:

Indiscriminate blasting of information to massive numbers of people has no benefit whatsoever. What you need to do is to distribute information selectively, to engage people with the right kind of information, to let them choose the information that is appropriate for them at that instant in time. That's the next major value point that we're going to see. That's why some of the technology information providers like Yahoo! have such a leverage point. They're already really hacking away at those critical problems about how to make appropriate information available to the appropriate people at the right time.

Another aspect of this selectivity, of course, is the security issue. Sometimes you want to be able to make the information available on a secure as well as a selective basis, and so you have to deal with that issue as well. But those are going to be refining technologies and opportunities for people who are creating new businesses on the Internet. Having a mechanism for being able to let people find very quickly what they want to find—that's the major problem that we're confronting now.

And it's actually being solved pretty well today. It's pretty amazing what you can find. For example, I went on a vacation in Canada recently and I knew before I left that I wanted to play golf, so I checked the Internet for the opportunities near the resort where I was staying. I got not only the golf courses in the area, but a whole series of user comments, collaborative comments, from a guest who had used those courses recently and reported that the greens weren't being very well maintained. This was very current and very personalized information that you could find in a matter of minutes, and only on the Net. So we've got a huge amount of stuff to filter through, but the tools are getting better, and I think that's where the real value is going to come—in continuing to make it easier and quicker for everyone to get this kind of specialized access.

Only the Internet does it in this branching, collaborative way. I go back 37 years in the industry to when we were trying to get access to information only in the batch mode and usually off of a paper tape or a card reader. To have information instantaneously available to millions of people simultaneously, with high bandwidth and high graphical resolution, is almost mind boggling.

What about the other beast lurking in the Internet jungle, the security threat? As John recognizes, the two problems—access and security—are connected. And he's fairly sanguine about our chances of resolving them:

Of course, you must have security in the application. That's going to be an absolute necessity. We've not been able to get around some of the fundamental problems of identifying who a person is and we're still using user ID's and passwords. But technologies for fingerprint recognition are going to help with that, and that's one of the products that Compaq offers right now. Compaq has a fingerprint security device that you can get as an enhancement to your PC. It reads your fingerprint to verify that you are who you say you are.

There are also security tools that are going to help. There's a company called Entrust that I think is going to be one of the major players. That's a Northern Telecom/Nortel spinout subsidiary that is going to be one of the key players in this security space. Another company called Tristrata has done some work that allows the encryption of information to occur at very, very high speeds—36 million bits per second—which means that you can encrypt a live video digital transmission in real time. These technologies, which allow the encryption of data and the management of secure tokens that are exchanged between trading partners, are going to make it increasingly possible to achieve the degree of security that businesses demand.

There's a lot of systems engineering work, a lot of implementation and execution work to be done to ensure that that is done properly, and it also is going to take some user acceptance to get to that degree of security. But it's a solvable problem—basically a set of engineering and instrumentation challenges—and the people who tackle it effectively are going to be the ones who win in this electronic commerce space.

A Final Word

If you're still wary about the security risks of E-business, you're not alone, and you're not necessarily paranoid. We've made good strides in keeping our firewalls secure, with encryption technology in particular getting better every day. But the war between hackers and good citizens is bound to continue, and there is much at stake.

If you have any doubt about the integrity of your networking system—and even the Pentagon isn't 100 percent sure about theirs—the practical advice is simple: Do a security audit. And do it as all audits should be done—on a regular basis.

You can do this internally or through outsourcing. For the former, you have a wide choice of off-the-shelf security tools, including Enterprise Security Manager from Axent Technologies;

Internet Security Scanner from Internet Security Systems; and NetSonar, from WheelGroup Corporation. Not too long ago, such hacker banes were, in the words of *Infoworld*, "immature and ornery. Just getting them to work required some pretty serious Unix expertise—as if the only dentist in town worked in an unmarked building, had no phone listing, and only gave diagnoses in Latin." Things have changed, and such tools are now easily adaptable to "normal network maintenance."

As for outsourcing, security checking is one of the Internet's great growth segments, and the news for the company IS manager is good indeed. IBM alone offers hacker-blocking services that range from a $5,000 workshop to a $120,000 analysis, and they are only one player in a competitive field. Another name to watch is International Network Services, whose consultancy services might run from $80,000 to $300,000, depending on the size of the firm and the complexity of the audit.

"Information is power," Deborah Radcliff writes in *Infoworld*. "It is the hacker creed. If your company stores any valuable information on your Web servers and those servers are housed at an ISP or Web housing center, you should pay close attention to your ISP's security policy." That goes as well for your own, on both sides of the firewall.

In a world of cybermischief, that is common sense.

Chapter 3

Lessons of the First Generation

The Internet has brought about an unparalleled business opportunity. But, as with any great opportunity, there are palpable risks, as hundreds of Netrepreneurs establish online footholds every week, and as the protocols of the E-business game are still changing daily. It's an exciting world, but its newness and complexity also make it a hazardous one.

To avoid the hazards and capitalize on the opportunities, you need to make the transition from conventional to electronic business with a savvy blend of exuberance and deliberation. Going too slow—or failing to recognize the revolutionary potential of the Net—may mean that you will miss a millennial watershed in economic history. Going too fast—rushing onto the field without learning the rules—can get you trampled in the ongoing stampede of enthusiastic Netwits whose Web sites, all graphic bells and whistles, have no strategic pull.

Throughout the rest of this book, we'll give specific strategies and examples of how to navigate the Internet waters effectively. But let's start with some general observations. Here are some basic lessons of E-business's first generation—the most fundamental of the cyber rules that we've learned so far.

Lesson 1: "Zapping" Is the Way of the Web

Remember the sheer volume of information that is already out there in cyberspace, beckoning for your customers' attention. This may seem obvious, but it bears emphasis because its historical uniqueness represents a difference not just of degree but of kind.

Net business volume, which is to say the volume of potential choices that a customer may make over the Net, is a function not of quantity alone but of quantity enhanced by an incredibly fast navigability. The real reason that online business is so novel, and so competitive, is not just the magnitude of the infinite marketplace, but the speed with which your customers can move around within it—and out of it—at the click of a mouse.

In a traditional market, the guiding metaphor is location, or *place*. Since the days of the ancient Greek agora, merchants and customers have transacted business in geographically defined areas called marketplaces, and we have carried that metaphor dutifully into this century, applying it even to transactions where some of the players are in Chicago and others in Hong Kong. It has remained an appropriate metaphor because, even when business is conducted over great distances, the negotiations are still finalized, deals are still struck, at one or more discernible points on the physical planet.

Customers weighing purchasing options are likewise constrained by place. In the simplest on-the-ground transactions, the agora variety, the customer has to physically leave one car dealer and drive to get to another. But even in the relatively unconstrained models of phone and television home shopping, place is a factor. The customer still has to disconnect from one 800 number and dial another, or request a brochure to be reviewed at another time and place. In the speediest of pre-Net transactions, there's still a phone-to-phone (or order form to order department) linkage between company and customer, and that linkage is both place-specific and relatively slow.

The Net changes that. Sitting at a PC with his or her hand on a mouse, today's customer can access a virtually limitless range of purchasing possibilities. To companies, this presents a tremendous marketing challenge. The Internet's challenge is not like that of a mere superstore. If it were, electronic malls would be the darlings of the medium, instead of the erratic phenomenon that they actually are. The Internet's value is that it is a store in which place has no meaning, and in which, therefore, you can move from "aisle" to "aisle" in a rapid and *discontinuous* fashion.

The rapidity itself is revolutionary, but it's the discontinuity that is truly unparalleled. Between the Greek agora and today's giant malls, customers considered their choices in a continuous pattern: They walked (or thought) step by step from the wine to the grapes to the carpets to the blenders to the modems. With Net technology, they can now surf from the wine to the modems to a Jane Austen discussion group to a Beach Boys memorabilia site before the traditional shopper has gotten her wine to the checkout

counter. The logic of shopping in this medium is completely cus-
tomer-controlled, and the decisions that he or she makes about
purchasing, not purchasing, or leaving the store entirely are instantaneous and incontestable. They happen at "whim speed."

For companies accustomed to demonstrating the value of their
products or solutions to "rational optimizing actors," this is a
monumental change in purchasing pattern. In fact, Internet technology has the ability nearly to obliterate pattern, by facilitating
the cyberspace surfing that techies call "zapping." To a business
professional trying to get his or her products seriously considered
on the Web, zapping is a warp speed version of "just browsing,"
the electronic counterpart of every retailer's pet peeve. And, far
from being an incidental annoyance, it's the Web way of life.

Lesson 2: Direct Traffic Aggressively

The combination of infinite choice and whim speed puts an interesting spin on advertising, since your potential customers online are going to be active, not passive, recipients of your Web site
messages. Any prospective purchaser of your products who is
looking at your company on a PC screen has *chosen* to do so. Unlike the traditional passive recipient of a billboard or TV message,
online prospects have actively clicked on your information; that
is, pulled it off the Internet through a search box or hyperlink.
Your first order of business is to get them to do that. It's to increase the probability that, out of the millions of URLs available
to them, they will be inexorably drawn to yours.

What will encourage prospective customers to click on your
URL—that is, to "hit" your Web site—is the same combination

of broadcasting and target marketing that spells success (if you do it right) in any advertising medium.

Think in terms of the overused image of the Internet as an information superhighway. Your Web site address is accessible through a single "off-ramp"—one of literally millions—and your challenge as a marketer is to get your customers to take that off-ramp rather than another. How? By putting the image of your off-ramp in your customers' minds as vividly and as frequently as you can. In doing this, the savviest Net marketers use both off-line and online advertising.

Off-line advertising means the traditional print and electronic media that advertisers have been using for a century. Placing a Web site address at the bottom of a magazine ad, within a television commercial, or on a billboard is an effective and relatively inexpensive way of alerting people to your digital outreach. Already, URL addresses are nearly as ubiquitous in public spaces and on business cards as 800 numbers were a decade ago. Augmenting your traditional advertising by adding such addresses is the most commonsense way for a digitizing business to broadcast the message, "The next time you're on the Internet, check us out."

A newer, more expensive, and yet essential ingredient in the "directing traffic" mix is online advertising. There are three essential venues for doing this: search engines, industry-specific "hub sites," and "gateway" ads.

Search engines, sometimes called "directories," are the most frequently visited Web sites on the Internet, because they are many Web users' first port of call. Getting your company site listed in one or more of these entry vehicles is therefore a must for any serious Net marketer. Search engines are like the Yellow Pages of the Net. Net users, whether they're highly focused prospects or whimsical zappers, commonly begin by feeding their search engines essential keywords (like the top-of-the-page categories in the Yellow Pages), and it is through these keywords that the user will be directed to your company. The choice of such keywords is therefore of great importance, and should be carefully thought out as part of your application for directory listings.

Among the best-known search engines today are Yahoo!, AltaVista, Infoseek, Excite, Lycos, and Magellan. All of these link to company Web sites, but also to anything else anybody searching the Net might want to find. Thus their very advantage is also their limitation. They make no distinction between business and non-business interests. A customer seeking information on Lycos about the Mr. Turkey company, for example, may have to ferret that information out from reams of data on turkey raising, the folklore of Thanksgiving, and the news from Istanbul.

Because the major search engines are so bewilderingly comprehensive, you might also want to list your Web site on a purely commercial directory such as the Commercial Sites Index (at *www.directory.net)* or on an industry hub site. *Hub sites* afford you the opportunity to pull from a more focused clientele—users who have already navigated to your general field of operation, and who are seeking more specific information about you and your competitors. While industry hub sites have less overall traffic than general search engines, that traffic is dedicated. Of the Net's numerous dedicated hub sites, a representative sampling would include sites for catalog companies *(www.catalogsite.com)*, car dealerships *(www.dealer.net)*, insurance firms *(www.insurancenet. com)*, and hotels *(www.hotelnet.co.uk)*.

A third strategy is to purchase *gateway ads*—advertising space, in the form of hyperlink buttons, on Web sites where you suspect the traffic will contain prospective customers. Currently, the most popular sites for such ads are the major search engines: You'll see numerous across-the-screen hyperlinks, or "banner" advertisements, every time you click on Yahoo! or Excite. These are essentially off-ramp doorways for which the site owners pay Yahoo! or Excite a placement fee, and through which the user can navigate directly to the owner's own site.

Gateway ads may also be placed on related sites: The Mr. Turkey people, for example, might place one on pages devoted to Thanksgiving, menu planning, or poultry farming. In addition, a company may "sponsor" a related site. The baseball game site Fastball, for example, is supported by sponsorship fees from The Gap. If you click on *www.fastball.com* to play the game, you'll see that the screen representation of the outfield fence is plastered with Gap logos. It's an online version of a local restaurant sponsoring a Little League team.

Or take the case of the bakery Bagel Oasis. It has been (by its own estimation) "New York's favorite bagel shop for over three decades." A few years ago, seeing the opportunity in the Web, the family firm went online, and since then it has dramatically increased its reach from its Queens headquarters to customers as far afield as California and Maine. Bagel Oasis's core revenue comes from bagels, of course, but since it has been featured in *Business Week* and *New York* magazine stories, it has also managed to sell its own visibility by presenting itself as a billboard for related suppliers. Check out *www.bageloasis.com* and you will find, in addition to the bagels and company T-shirt offers, ad spots from Fine Southern Foods and Gifts, Genuine Smithfield Hams, and a Bagel Oasis customer, the Manhattan restaurant Balducci's. All of these attest to the power of visibility—and not so incidentally, help pay for the site.

Lesson 3: Be Seen at the Front Door

In the search for visibility, companies are also relying on a specialized form of long-term "watch this space" partnership. One leading player in this arena is America Online. With its growing millions of subscribers, AOL is the world's largest online service provider. In subscribing to AOL, these users get access to the Net at large, and also to the company's various proprietary services, offered through "channels" devoted to travel, finance, sports, kids, and so on. If you're an AOL subscriber, whatever you're looking for, your first stop is the AOL home page.

The service's frequent designation as one of the Web's most "popular" sites is thus a little misleading. It's popular in the same way that the front door of a museum is popular: Looking for Picasso? Pollack? Monet? It doesn't matter, because *every* AOL subscriber hits the front door first. In addition, the company's free site, at *www.aol.com*, gets its own tremendous share of online traffic, with nearly half of all Web consumers visiting it at least once a month. It's what the Internet community refers to as a "navigational hub" or "portal" site. These sites—the home pages of the major service providers and search engines—are consistently identified as the Web's most heavily traveled sites.

Because of this jumble at the portals, AOL has been able to market itself like prime billboard space. Preview Travel's category leadership has been due chiefly to great customer service, but its primacy was certainly not hampered when, in 1997, it arranged with AOL to be the only travel provider at that front door—at a cost of $32 million for a five-year exclusive contract.

The Preview deal was only one of many. In the six months following its $32 million agreement, several other businesses also established portal visibility:

- In a multimillion-dollar deal in October 1997, American Greeting Corporation closed a three-year contract to develop electronic greeting cards on both the subscription and public segments of the AOL service.
- That December, under the gun from upstart Amazon.com, Barnes & Noble became AOL's exclusive online bookseller, a privilege for which the ante was $40 million over four years.
- In January 1998, Cyberian Outpost Inc. signed a $5 million, one-year deal to be AOL's third-party retailer of computer hardware.
- That February, Intuit Inc.—makers of the Quicken financial planning program—agreed to pay $30 million over three years for AOL portal exclusivity in the area of financial programming.

The Intuit deal in particular was a directional indicator. Personal finance is a hot topic on the Web, and AOL's personal-finance channel has long been among its most frequently visited features. "We manage 6 million portfolios for about 3 million subscribers on the service," AOL spokesman Tom Ziemba told journalist Bill Roberts just after the deal was closed. "In some areas—taxes, insurance, and home mortgages—Intuit had a stronger offering than we had." The deal specifically mandated those program offerings, as well as opening up the possibility that, if the alliance is effective, it could expand to include such Intuit trading partners as Charles Schwab.

The benefits of visibility should flow two ways, and that is clearly the case in the Intuit deal. In addition to the cash, AOL gets to expand its financial suite, while Intuit gains immediate access to a vast new audience. While the long-term, hoped-for benefit is more paying customers, the AOL-generated traffic is also a plus in itself, because it will enable Intuit to present its newly visible Web site as a good place for advertisers to heighten their *own* visibility.

In effect, Intuit was betting that much of that $30 million exposure fee would be offset by the higher rates it could now charge other companies to run banner and hyperlink ads on the Intuit Web site. Building on this belief, it later struck a deal with Excite—a search engine hub with a viewership rivaling that of Netscape. The hope behind such deals—and it's a sensible one—is that, in the graphics-heavy whirlwind of Internet commerce, visibility is both an entry fee and its own reward.

But is it clear that this is true?

In 1997, seeking an answer to that question, the market research firm Millward Brown Interactive conducted the largest ad-effectiveness study ever done in any medium. Focusing on twelve heavy-traffic sites including CNN, Excite, and Pathfinder, MBI demonstrated that banner ads there not only significantly increased brand awareness but had a measurable "positive impact on intent to purchase."

Based on their research methodology, Millward Brown Interactive is now offering an online service called Voyager, which allows marketers to utilize a panel of representative Web users, along with a suite of ad-effectiveness tools, to track the on-site flow of potential customers and measure the likely pull of specific communications. They are also selling an add-on application for ad servers that gauges the value of particular ads on particular sites. Clearly, businesses are way beyond putting up billboards all over cyberspace and hoping that browsers will somehow get their messages.

Lesson 4: Give More Than "Brochureware"

Once you've got prospective customers to visit your site, how do you keep them there long enough to make a sale? How do you minimize what one Internet analyst calls "clickitis"?

The answers depend on who the prospects are and what you want them to do during their visit. One of the first lines of defense against clickitis—and one that is often overlooked—is to offer visitors some immediate compensation for spending time there. When users click on your home page, they've given you a "quo." If you're not pretty quick with a "quid," they may zap themselves elsewhere.

Again, this departs from the traditional market model. When you phone or write a company for product information, what you typically receive is an illustrated brochure and an order form. That's acceptable (barely) in analog shopping, but not in cyberspace. Compared to the typical predigital customer, the typical online browser is more impatient, quicker on the trigger, and far more demanding. You cannot hold his attention with electronic "brochureware." If that was all the compensation he was looking for, he could get it through the mail.

What are E-customers looking for? First of all, quality information. A good Web site presents much more than a graphical representation of its printed literature. It offers potential customers "thick description."

We borrow this term from philosopher Gilbert Ryle, who applies it to analyses of human behavior that address not just surface meanings (the "thin" aspect of behavior), but the entire multilayered texture of sociocultural context—what anthropologist

Clifford Geertz, in a famous assessment of Ryle, calls the "piled-up structures of inference and implication." It's those piled-up structures that Web users demand. A good Web page makes the description of what it's offering as thick as possible.

For example, consider two winners of the annual Tenagra Awards for Internet Marketing Excellence. Virtual Vineyards, run by brothers-in-law Peter Granoff and Robert Olson, sells wine, food, and related products to an upscale clientele. Ragú uses the Net to get feedback from its customers and to increase brand awareness. But as different as the companies are in their business models and customer bases, they have been equally successful in applying "thick description" to their online presence.

Visitors to the Virtual Vineyard home page *(www.virtualvin. com)* may choose to go directly to order options, read one of several feature stories, peruse detailed and witty descriptions of possible purchases, download recipes, or explore interactive "fun stuff" under the categories "Ask the Cork Dork," "Ask the Food Dude," and "Ask the Recipe Queen." There's plenty of opportunity for visitors to set up accounts, e-mail the company, and make purchases, but these functional aspects are enveloped in such a pleasantly gustatory ambiance that merely browsing the site seems a sensory experience. By "thickening" the site with wine-related information, and by facilitating viewer interaction through regular features, Granoff and Olson have transformed their virtual environment into a credible replica of a wine-and-cheese gathering—a roomful of friendly, passionate, and well-informed enthusiasts. In other words, they've brought together (or rather created) that community of like-minded souls that all marketers dream of capturing.

The same is true of the Ragú site, which is less tony but no less enthusiastic. Click on *www.eat.com* and you will be ushered into the virtual home of "Mama Cucina," a gray-haired charmer who dispenses, along with recipes, such gastronomic witticisms as "Life is uncertain; eat dessert first" and "Gossip is good for your digestion." Everything at this user-friendly site circles, with disarming freshness, around Italian food, so that the product message is as indirect as it is pervasive. Mama Cucina's kitchen doesn't have to sell product directly because the entire thrust of the graphics is to send you scurrying to the store.

Click on the recipes, for example, and you will find that, except for the items on Mama's ample dessert tray, it is evidently impossible to cook anything without Ragú sauce. Click on "Goodies," and you will be offered T-shirts and Blockbuster tickets as premiums in exchange for Ragú proofs-of-purchase. Click on "Learn Italian" and you will be exposed to "Professor Antonio," whose phrase book favors such gems as "Can I have thirds of that pasta?" The site even has a running soap opera, whimsically entitled *As the Lasagna Bakes*. As with Virtual Vineyards, the drivers are thick description and a sense of community.

Unlike Virtual Vineyards, Ragú doesn't even attempt to sell its products over the Internet. It doesn't have to—and this is an important lesson for businesses going digital. As we mentioned in the first chapter, the single greatest benefit that retailers are now enjoying from expanding to the Internet is enhancement of their brand recognition.

Thick description addresses your customers' objective needs. Experience shows that you must also satisfy their subjective needs by providing "flow," that is, the experience of *fluid interaction*. Evan Schwartz, author of *Webonomics*, refers to this quality when he observes that many potential customers treat the Web as "a place where they can interact with other people."

The most effective Web sites are not just billboards on the side of the road. They are more like a place where everybody knows your name—even if it's not your real name. The information, or content, can become the centerpiece of their conversations. But it's the total experience that compels people to return to that place again and again.

You can see this principle at work in both the Virtual Vineyards and the Ragú sites; and also in such other high-interaction sites as the well-known Amazon.com virtual book mall *(www. amazon.com)*, which aims for the relaxing hubbub of a small-town bookstore. In all these sites, it's the experience of "flow," as much as the hard data, that keeps the viewers from succumbing to clickitis.

We live in a world which, in spite of interconnectedness, is perceived as atomized; linked to everything amorphously, we hunger for the concrete. The best of today's Web technologies take advantage of this irony. The best corporate Web pages, too, provide their viewers not just "hard" information but the "softer" attraction of virtual face time, of one-to-one interactivity, that is the subjective sine qua non for visitor retention. This explains why so many ostensible business pages are full of games, chat rooms, contests, and product-related trivia.

And while you're thinking about giving more than brochureware, consider the related strategy of giving something away. Not the entire store, but something. This principle, which strikes many traditional businesspeople as anathema, can be a critical leverage point on the World Wide Web. Because of the virtually unlimited choices it presents to users, the culture of the Web is built on the promise of "freedom," and this means that Web consumers, far more than comparable target markets, are reluctant to pay cover charges for looking around. That's why many successful marketers drop those entry fees and offer basic services as electronic loss leaders.

Logos, an Italian translation company, has been excelling on the Web since 1995. With a staff of 1,200 translators, it produces over 200 translations a day for a client base that began with small Italian manufacturers and that now includes such high-tech giants as Sun Microsystems and Texas Instruments. Such clients pay a premium price for the company's multilingual expertise and—thanks to Web-based e-mail—its quick turnaround time. But Logos also relies on the "freebie" principle.

The company dictionary, which founder Rodrigo Vergara describes as "our collective memory," contains five million entries in more than thirty languages. It was built up over the years by the translators themselves, who are required to submit a glossary along with each new translation. The database continues to grow by 500 terms a day. Anyone—Logos customer or not—can access it free.

On the company's Web page you can also link to "Wordtheque," where book citations allow you to see a word in context, and access Word Exchange Forum, an electronic version of a linguist's Notes and Queries. As Vergara explained to the *New York Times,* the open forum is a place where his staff and the public can interact on an informal, no–cover charge basis. "We won't translate a full text for free, of course, but if you can't find a word or, say, need to know a proverb in another language, you can ask for assistance in our forum and our translators—or other Web users—will try to help you."

Logos's multilingual database cost the company about $1 million to put online. Yet giving it away has clearly been a plus for the company. "The site is being used in schools, by professionals, and even by competitors," says Vergara. "This gives us a very high profile—and attracts new customers worldwide."

Another giveaway example is software producer Starwave, bankrolled by Microsoft cofounder Paul Allen and its media partner ESPN. Of its several online enterprises, its biggest revenue producer, ESPN SportsZone, makes money by a judicious blend of purchase offers and giveaways. According to publicist Jennifer Yazzolino, SportsZone is a subscription service that is "tiered so you can get stuff for free but the really hard-core fans buy stuff they can't get somewhere else."

That specialty "stuff" includes a premium subscription service called ESPN Insider, branded merchandise, and membership in ESPN-managed rotisserie leagues. Money from these upper-tier offerings, in addition to advertising revenues, keeps the site viable, so that it is able to offer the bulk of its service, a massive hoard of sports-related statistics, without charge. But it's the free access to that information that brings browsers to SportsZone in the first place—and that positions them to become paying customers. Thanks to this tiering strategy, SportsZone has become one of the hottest sites in the Internet universe. In 1995, the site was building toward 100,000 visits a day; less than three years later, that number had jumped to 650,000.

The best examples of the freebie strategy are in software products—the products that facilitate Internet usage itself. A major case in point is the giveaway of browsers—a practice that back in the dark ages (that is, three years ago) was standard operating procedure.

Netscape started the trend in 1995, when it gave away millions of copies of its Netscape Navigator, thus capturing (for a while) a near monopoly of the infant user market. But just as Netscape was entering the transition to a pay-for-business model—charging customers $49 for an upgraded Navigator—in strode Microsoft's Bill Gates to announce the same freebie policy that Netscape was abandoning.

Retailers have used loss leaders for most of this century. In a competitive environment like the Web, the "free entry" principle is bound to remain the standard for some time to come. Indeed, it may get even better (from the consumer's standpoint), as companies engage in new battles to "out-freebie" one another as a means of getting visitors, who may later become paying customers, through their electronic doors.

Lesson 5: Think Convenience

According to an old selling adage, the art of selling is making it easy for your customers to buy. On the WWW, where the easiest thing of all is to click away, good companies observe this rule in two related ways.

First, they provide an online product or service that is seen by their customers as more convenient than the brick-and-mortar alternatives. All of us today are packing forty-eight-hour schedules into twenty-four-hour days, and we are looking desperately for anything that will cut down on the frenzy. So if you do something for your customers that will save them time—that will thin out even a few routine items from their overstuffed inboxes—they will reward you with their business and their loyalty, even if it means paying a premium price. That was a major lesson taught by the catalog companies, and it's one of the lessons that migrates well to the Web: If you give people back their time, they will give you their money.

Consider Streamline, a shopping service based in Westwood, Massachusetts. It offers a complete online shopping system, including a sophisticated capability of creating preference files. When you sign up with Streamline, which offers dry cleaning and video rental in addition to groceries, a company employee visits your home and scans in all the food you have on your shelves using a bar-code reader. This, and an initial interview that records your preferences (green or ripe bananas, whole wheat or white bread, red or black caviar) provides the basis for a household buying profile.

You also receive a patented "service box" located in your garage or basement where it can be accessed via a keypad entry system. Any foods you order via an online catalog, or any scheduled automatic deliveries, are placed in this service box, where they can stay fresh for up to twenty-four hours. Dry cleaning and video rentals are also delivered to and picked up from the box, and all of it is controlled through the Web, making it an efficient as well as a convenient way to shop.

By making it quicker for people to do something that they had to do (or wanted to do) anyway, numerous online businesses have traded time for money, and come out ahead. This principle explains, for example, the success of the major delivery services, FedEx and UPS; the emergence of digital stock brokerages like E*TRADE; and the expansion of digital financial services like Charles Schwab online. In all of these cases, virtuality empowers visitors by making it easier for them to get what they want. The natural trajectory here is toward greater self-service. "Helping investors," as the Schwab slogan says, "to help themselves." Substitute "customer" for "investor" and you've got a good handle on how the first generation of digital capitalists are leveraging convenience. They have to. They know that, other things being equal, customers will always take the path of least resistance.

That is true as well with regard to the other half of the convenience equation: the ease that you've got to offer your customers once they're online. Here is where companies can really capitalize on timesaving technology—and where many of them, because they misunderstand that technology, drop the ball. This is ironic as well as sad, because it does you no good to sell your Web site as the easy alternative if your customers find navigating around it like a slog through molasses.

Making it convenient for your customers to use your Web site is a matter, when you come right down to it, of Web site design. We'll speak more about this in Chapter 11, but for now just think of "good design" as a synonym for "ease of navigability." On an effectively designed Web site, you always know exactly where you are, and it's crystal clear how to get from there to anywhere else, because every page gives unambiguous links to the other pages. In addition, you can navigate the whole site quickly and without backtracking. A good site never violates the three-click rule ("Users will not stay on-site if it takes more than three clicks to access the information they need"), and it tells the visitor at the front door (the "splash," or home page) exactly what's inside.

Paradoxically but predictably, a well-designed page may be less "distinctive" than a poorly designed one. It's like Tolstoy's famous quip. Every unhappy family is unhappy in its own way, while the happy families seem to be all alike. Similarly, when you visit a "happy" Web site, there may be nothing noticeably special about it: As on every other good site, it's just easy to get around. On a miserable site, however, you'll know something's different. You'll know because you're rattling back and forth like your steering wheel is broken.

Here's an example. A friend of ours who attended a big university is considering going back to school for a graduate degree. Recently she accessed the Web site of her alma mater in an attempt to secure some copies of her undergraduate transcript. The site came up fine, but that's about all. No matter what keywords she typed into the "search" function—transcripts, records, registrar—she could find no online information to help her solve her problem. Eventually she resorted to snail mail. That's bad design.

As an example of great design, check out the Novell site at *www.novell.com.* The front page gives a clear and comprehensive menu, so that whether you're looking for the corporate mission, the company structure, or product options, getting there is clearly marked, and only a click away. If you're interested in exploring Novell solutions, moreover, you'll find a "solutions" page that is eminently user-friendly. It offers a series of commonly asked questions to help you pinpoint your problem, and then hyperlinks you directly to the appropriate Novell solution. A customized response within seconds—that's good design.

Lesson 6: Close the Loop

On the Internet, you've got to be on guard against unintended consequences. Volvo, in opening up its Web site a few years ago, found that out when an e-mail function that it had hoped would elicit fan mail became instead a conduit for owner complaints. As Bob Austin, the company's director of U.S. marketing, noted, "People would occasionally write things like: 'Nice Web site, but

the sun roof on my 850 leaks.' " Product liability laws require responses to such complaints, yet Volvo had failed to anticipate
their volume, and was underprepared to field them from its headquarters. Eventually, the e-mail feature had to be deleted, for it
had opened a door into the company that could not be properly
monitored.

The lesson? The most attractive Web site in the world cannot
manage its own traffic. When you invite people into your business
by going on the Web, you are in effect opening an electronic circuit. The circuit has to be closed from within a home office, or
some other office specifically designated to handle the increased
flow. If you don't do that—if you don't establish internal processes
to make the site truly *interactive*—the sequence of your Web site
activity is going to go from curiosity to frustration to irritation,
with the end result being a loss of potential business.

Similar problems can affect even Net-savvy companies. Daniel
Leemon, chief strategy officer at the Charles Schwab Corporation, describes what happened to the customer-service capabilities of this online pioneer when a sudden surge of activity
overloaded the system.

> The telephone has been around for 100 years, so we all under-
> stand a busy signal or a hold message. It's different with the In-
> ternet. During the great Wall Street storm of October 1997, for
> example, when the market went down 500 points in one day
> and up 200 the next day, our site and many others were over-
> whelmed. At that time we didn't have a message to alert in-
> vestors that they were in a queue, and as a result many of them
> became frustrated. They didn't know where they were or
> whether they'd get through.

That's a rare case, but it's indicative of issues that have yet to be completely worked out. The most interesting complexity today is the stress testing that the Internet hasn't yet been through. We've quadrupled our capacity to make sure this doesn't happen again, and, if it ever does, we'll put a clearer description of what's happening up on the screen.

Quadrupling your capacity, of course, doesn't come free. Neither do other adjustments, which might include revamping your order function, retraining your customer service people, or dedicating significant resources toward upgrading your customer database. But if you want your Web site to serve as a true connector to your customers, such back-office improvements are not optional. When you go digital, you're making a quantum leap in your corporate reach. You're casting a much wider net, if you will. If you don't strengthen your corporate boat at the same time, you can easily get swamped by a marvelous catch. That's why the establishment of a Web-based invitation can be only one element in an integrated marketing strategy.

In our business of sales and marketing technology, this integration of front- and back-office functions is well established. When a customer calls Siebel Systems, whether the call has been prompted by our Web site, a print or electronic advertisement, or previous customer contact, our call center staff enters the incoming information into our automated customer management system, along with any responses, referrals, or other "to dos" (also automated) that might have to be handled by another staff person or department. Through enterprise-wide database management, constantly updated, we are able to maintain highly detailed profiles on our customers, to ensure that, whatever "door" they choose to knock (or click) on, a well-informed employee will be there to respond to their needs.

We call this kind of automated information flow a "closed loop" system. It's at the heart of every effective sales and marketing structure. It should also be at the heart of your Web site planning.

Lesson 7: Don't Go It Alone

Strategic alliances are becoming critical to corporate survival, and nowhere is this more vivid than on the World Wide Web. What we are seeing there, according to some analysts, is the beginning of the end of vertical integration and the rise of a collaborative model called "virtual integration." Increasingly, successful companies are coming to understand that continued success must be leveraged against interlocking resources, and that the days of the lone-wolf company are coming to an end.

Take Ariba Technologies, Inc. Having developed an online procurement system whose clients included such business heavyweights as Cisco Systems and VISA, Ariba recently brought together a consortium of equally successful specialists to create a soup-to-nuts industrial procurement operation. Under this new multiplayer umbrella, Ariba's already effective operating resource management system will be enhanced by the shipping and warehousing expertise of FedEx, the data-management skills of Sterling Commerce, and an online payment process developed by VeriFone, experts in secure over-the-Net transmissions. Ariba client VISA will provide a unique purchasing card that, coupled with VeriFone's software, will add further security.

Why did they do this? Survival. As automation increases and E-business becomes more and more the order of the day, small firms like Ariba are obliged to extend their capabilities to meet the specific (and rapidly changing) requirements of corporate clients. Company president Keith Krach realized that they couldn't do this alone. As he told *Interactive Week*, "We understand that no individual company can automate the entire acquisition cycle and deliver open architectures for networked commerce, so we have partnered with leaders in key areas."

A similar attempt to extend reach was made by Classifieds2000. Based in Sunnyvale, California, Classifieds2000 runs online ads in nine categories, including real estate, jobs, and personals; business advertisers enable the company to pay its bills while continuing to offer free placements to private sellers.

Net-based classifieds have an inherent jump on print classifieds both because of the Internet's international audience and because of the computer-based system's quick search abilities. As Classifieds2000's VP for marketing, Karim El-Fishawy, says, "You can find what you're looking for quickly because you can tell the computer exactly what you want—no more shuffling through pages and pages of a newspaper." Classifieds2000 capitalized on that advantage by forging partnerships with over 130 other sites, including Microsoft's WebTV and major search engines like Lycos and Infoseek. The synergistic result has been a torrent of users. According to El-Fishawy, the site gets more than 2.5 million viewers every day.

Both of these partnering examples are true Web phenomena. They're not simply migrations of existing partnerships onto the Web but synergistic alliances formed within, and in a sense only made possible by, the revolutionary interactivity of the Web environment. That is one of the exciting things about E-business—its capacity for transforming the basic rules of the game.

Lesson 8: Improve as You Go

It has been established business wisdom for centuries that, in starting or building a business, you should have a clear idea of where you're going before you step out. That principle is being radically challenged by the speed of Net innovation. In the Net world, product cycles have become so short that conventional caution can sometimes be a liability. Rather than "Beta your way to success," the operating wisdom today is "Get it in the water now," or what Internet publisher Chuck Martin calls "launch and learn."

The "launch" part—the sense that it's better to float something than to have a perfect vessel in drydock—is the logical response to Moore's Law. Gordon Moore, the cofounder of Intel, formulated this principle in the 1970s, when his infant company was developing the now ubiquitous microprocessor. Moore's Law states that the speed, size, and cost of microprocessors—and, by implication, computer capability in general—tend to improve by a factor of two every eighteen months. In other words, whatever you're using today will be practically obsolete in little more than a year. That puts a tremendous competitive pressure on the industry as a whole. It also ensures increasing sophistication for process-hungry customers, and it makes "Launch it now" a virtual watchword. In the computer world, you simply can't afford to wait until everything's perfect. And the same principle applies to anyone considering going digital.

But launching without a commitment to learning is a guarantee of failure. Which is why it's important to remember that "on the fly" means not "wing it" but *improve as you go.* Get the ship out now, to be sure, but then assume that things will go wrong, and catch them before they do. The "launch and learn" principle may not be conservative, but it's not reckless, either. You can see that in the launch of the Walt Disney Company's online shopping site.

Given Disney's legendary obsession with perfect image, you might have expected the site to be a classic "every i dotted" affair. Actually, even though the site is far more elaborately tuned than most corporate Web sites, the company is fully committed to on-going tinkering. The site mission, says online commerce manager Russ Gillam, is to achieve the highest possible browser "conversion rate," that is, to turn every online "guest" into a purchaser. Since the average order at the online store is already double that of the average retail location, you'd think they'd be satisfied, but no. In his quest for even better numbers, Gillam captains a team of two dozen Web developers who are charged with generating constant improvements to the site.

So far they have helped to develop a handful of virtual boutiques, a navigational umbrella, shopping carts, personalized products, and a reward system for repeat buyers. Still in the works is a direct warehouse interface, which will automate fulfillment of orders within an hour of the visit. "Guest satisfaction will go up," Gillam predicted, "because they'll get packages faster." The site will also soon be able to access a product database to inform its virtual visitors about items that are temporarily out of stock. All in all, the store is an exemplary indication of how a constant dedication to fine-tuning can make a site more effective.

Lesson 9: E-Business Is Still Business

But effective for what? At the Disney shop, the answer is "higher conversion rates." But that's only one answer. It may or may not be the one that makes sense for you. Hence a final tip. Before you spend the resources that even an elementary Web site is going to cost you, define what you expect that presence to accomplish for your company.

If, like Disney, you want to actually sell products online, fine. Retailing, while far from being the hottest (that is, most success-ful) aspect of E-business at this point, still offers tremendous opportunities. But if that's your goal, take a tip from the most suc-cessful online retailers. Establish a clear and steady link between your back office and your electronic "door," and listen to what your customers are telling you about what works and what doesn't.

If, like Ragú, you're not interested in direct sales but in build-ing goodwill and brand recognition, that's fine, too. But remem-ber that on the intensively interactive Web, you do that not merely by trumpeting your name and logo but by *associating* them with Ryle's "thick description." This has as much to do with cre-ating a brand-rich ambience—a subjective atmosphere—as it does with providing a texture of brand information.

Direct sales and brand enhancement are probably the two most common uses that corporations have so far made of the Web, but there are others, and it is in the nature of the Web that new uses of the medium will be found as time goes on. The import house Pier One and the office supply firm Staples, for example, run Web sites that do little more than direct interested customers to their local outlets. They serve as dispatchers for customers who are already familiar with their brands.

There's nothing right or wrong about any of these strategic choices. The point is to be clear about what your mission is up front. What gets Web novices in trouble is expecting the medium to deliver a corporate return that the structure of the business has not been designed to respond to. If that sounds like basic business savvy, it is. In a sense, that's the most important principle of all. Let us illustrate with the story of a famous Web disaster.

Nets Inc. started out in Pittsburgh in 1990 as Automation New Network. Founded by Donald Jones, the company provided magazines containing the latest industrial news, and every six months it produced an industry directory. This business was intended to be the forerunner of an electronic clearinghouse for manufacturing news and products. Customers were to be connected to the company by an electronic pager through which they could download information, but the connection was too expensive to create. In 1990, Jones saw his chance to make this concept real by using the low-cost technology of the Web as a replacement for the pager. By the end of 1995, he had transferred his magazine and product information to the Web, and was generating about $2 million in monthly fees from vendors whose catalogs he was posting online.

Although the Web site was successful, taking the next step to E-business required more cash. Late in 1995, Jones managed to obtain the attention of Hambrecht & Quist LLC, a high-tech investment concern, which invested $15 million in the business. To protect its money, H&Q believed it needed visibility on Wall Street, which meant bringing in a well-known name to help run the company. They picked software executive Jim Manzi, who had helped bring Lotus Development to prominence.

Jones's dream was to get a jump on business-to-business e-commerce, establish a central position in a huge industry, and gather large revenues from membership and transaction fees. Much of the appeal of the company was the promise that participation would allow members, through some magical benefit of e-commerce that was never explained, to double their profits. Everyone "knew" that business-to-business commerce was going to suddenly kick into a sudden growth curve, dramatically outperforming the general consumer market.

But there were problems, starting with Manzi's insensitivity to rising expenses and his software focus in a business that wasn't software. The fact that his software developers missed almost every release schedule dramatically accelerated the demise of the company. Add this to the fact that he planned to expand Nets Inc. into travel and pharmacy before capturing a leadership position in its existing market, and you can anticipate the company's sinking fortunes. A year after Manzi joined, revenues had sunk from $2 million per month to $85,000 a month. The company struggled on until May 1997, when it finally closed its doors.

The fundamental reason that this happened was that Manzi and Jones had had blind faith in the timely inevitability of e-commerce. Convinced that it would provide them with a constantly growing customer base, regardless of what they did, they focused on technology when they should have focused on customer satisfaction, and behaved as if they were immune to the normal laws of business. But E-business is still *business*. Electronic customers are still customers. If you forget this, you do so at your peril.

If your customers aren't happy with you at the end of the day, it won't make any difference whether you sold product to them through the Web or hand-carried it to their doorstep. If you can't support them, they will leave you for a vendor that can. If they gain no advantage from an association with you, then they will select vendors who offer full partnerships and lasting relationships.

It isn't about the "E" in E-business. It's about providing value to the customer. In all the hoopla, Manzi and Jones forgot that. But their customers didn't.

Lesson 10: Yes, You Can

The final lesson is an objection to be overcome. Because many of the Internet's most famous first generation stories come from extremely large and extremely successful global enterprises, you may be tempted to assume that this space isn't for you—especially if your own business is a small or local one. Overcoming that antipathy is an imperative, because the principles of the giants' successes *are* generalizable. Any doubts you may have about that quickly disappear in the face of the facts. Here's the reality, for example, behind three of the most common reservations.

"E-business is too expensive for me to roll out in my company." Yes, it costs money. But you've got to spend money to make money and, all things considered, investing in Net-based business can be extraordinarily cost-effective. The chief information officer of giant Cisco, Pete Solvik, estimates that it costs his company less than $10 million per year to maintain its E-business infrastructure, with about $50 million having been required for initial capital outlay. Considering Cisco's financial return, those are small numbers. If you're smart, you'll scale your E-business technology to fit your requirements. Keep it small, and do what is appropriate for your business.

"It will be a cultural shock for my managers and sales force. I'll never get it in place." New ideas always encounter resistance, but if you think that cultural shock is a sufficient reason to keep off the Web, think again. The fact is, the culture shift has already happened: Cisco CEO John Chambers himself has pointed out that soon one quarter of all *small* businesses will be online, with probably twice that percentage among medium businesses. When you understand that, you mandate culture change in your company, or you watch that company become part of a cultural backwash. It'll work if you want it to, and if you involve those who participate in the resulting successes.

"My customers are used to their existing ways of doing things." No doubt. But they're also asking you, loud and clear, to help them change. Your customers are ready for E-business now. They're waiting for you to show the way, hoping to share in the mutual success that an online strategy will bring. Leaders like Cisco, Compaq, and Charles Schwab are able to provide high-quality personalized support to many more customers now than they could before they used the Internet. This translates directly to increased customer satisfaction. Their revenues are also much higher than they were before they went digital, and their business partners benefit directly and indirectly from that fact.

Increased revenues, increased operating efficiencies, lower costs, happier customers. Whatever your business and whatever your size, that's a blueprint that no savvy company can ignore.

Part II

On the Horizon

E-Business's Cyber Rules

Chapter 4

Private "Infotainment" Will Give Way to Global Enterprise

One of the early misconceptions about the Internet was that it was going to be a playground for the illiterate. Social critic Neil Postman, in a 1993 attack on "Future Schlock" for the *Toronto Globe and Mail*, warned that the new technology's chief purpose was to expand the available smorgasbord of "infotainment," that is, to supply directionless and self-absorbed consumers with an ever expanding array of situation comedies, light news, and game shows.

Few businesspeople, even in 1993, took this kind of sniping very seriously, but the technophobic attitude that it embodies has been a persistent factor in discussions of the medium, and it has contributed greatly to the depiction of cyberspace activity as simultaneously diverting and anarchic. This characterization has made the Internet seem to the unsophisticated like the proper home not of business but of fun and games.

That is changing now, and changing fast. The emergence of the Web as a quintessential *business* medium is the first and one might say the most obvious trend that now confronts everyone who wants to spend time there. No one, as has often been said, actually owns the Web, and legally that's certainly true. But if anyone may claim de facto ownership, it is not entertainment purveyors but enterprise managers.

A small but significant sign of this enterprise dominance may be seen in the legal battles over registering domain names.

Who Owns Your Company's Name?

Common sense, and the logic of search engines, say you should pick a domain name that reflects either the name of your company or the nature of your business. If you're Diamond Inc. and you manufacture lightbulbs, go for *www.diamond.com* or *www.lightbulbs.com*. Good rule, but up until now—because of the residual power of an "infotainment" attitude—it has not always been observable. Because the Network Information Center and Network Solutions, Inc., the governing body for domain name registration, have long been accepting names on a first-come, first-served basis, your ideal name may very well have already been taken—and not necessarily by another "Diamond" or lightbulb manufacturer.

Many famous brand names and slogans have been spoken for by their manufacturers, so that when you go to *www.whopper. com*, *www.pampers.com*, and *www.justdoit.com*, you will in fact end up on the Burger King, Procter & Gamble, and Nike sites. But other "obvious" addresses turn up surprises. The Coca-Cola Company, for example, is fighting to gain possession of *www.coke.com,* but as of now it's registered to Rajeev Arora. The McDonald's Corporation owns *www.mcdonalds.com,* but it had to buy the privilege from the initial owner, Joshua Quittner, by making a donation to his favorite school; they would love to own *www.bigmac.com* as well, but so far it's still in the hands of James McDonald. Tim Young owns *www.bandaid.com,* John Shelepet owns *www.jello.com,* and if you click on *www.abc.com,* you'll link not to the broadcasting giant but to ABC Design, an early-bird register from Seattle.

As if these legal "infringements" aren't already enough to drive corporate lawyers crazy, some companies have also had to contend with domain saboteurs. Until recently, the *www.ringling brothers.com* site was owned not by the famous circus but by the animal-rights activist organization People for the Ethical Treatment of Animals, who used it to condemn the mistreatment of circus elephants. In the spring of 1998, a court decision gave the name to Ringling Brothers, whereupon PETA moved to *www.circuses.com.* PETA itself, interestingly, had been the victim of name appropriation in 1996, when one Michael Doughney registered the name *www.peta.org* to publicize his satire "People Eating Tasty Animals." Network Solutions ruled that neither he nor PETA could use it, and as a result he formed the Domain Name Rights Coalition, which came to PETA's defense in the Ringling wrangle. Cyberspace makes strange bedfellows.

What all of this indicates, aside from the fact that the Net is full of free comedy, is an ongoing debate about whether the medium's "proper" role is chiefly communicative (that is, infotainment) or chiefly commercial. Domain name rights people, waving the First Amendment banner, argue that free speech should take precedence over trademark protection; the implicit values they defend (aside from the speculative value of owning the names) are libertarian, individual, and highly private.

Trademark owners, of course, have a different view, and the logic of the Net—not to mention common sense—is on their side. Although in the current era of "domain-o-mania" somebody else may already have staked out a company's claim to its own product names, in the near future these anomalies will subside. The role of the Net as a quintessential business engine—an engine of for-profit service to the public welfare—will totally eclipse its value as an entertainment vehicle. The result will be a historic shift from the private to the global.

A Globalizing Medium

You can see this dominance already, every time you log on to a PC and are greeted by an array of commercial messages. It's obvious, too, in Internet stock investment figures and in the emergence of companies like Yahoo! and Schwab and Cisco as experts in the fusion of technological and marketing innovations. No doubt noncommercial Net enthusiasts will continue to proliferate in cyberspace. But the future of the technology belongs to business. The linkage of the World Wide Web and the global economy is as much a natural marriage as the nineteenth-century linkage between railroads and corporations.

When we say global, we mean just that. Although the first generation of Internet commerce has been dominated by U.S. enterprises, the inclusion of the rest of the planet is inevitable, because the economy itself is so globalized.

First to be involved in this development will be European firms. Although there is still some skepticism among U.S. observers about European Internots, as well as some European reluctance about seizing the new technology, the consensus among European executives is very clear: They are bidding, now, to be major players in the Internet space. "There is no longer a lag in Europe's understanding of the opportunities provided by the Net," said one European manufacturing executive last year. "We get it; we're over the initial confusion."

The uptake so far has been hampered by limited infrastructure and the slow pace of telecom deregulation, but European executives are generally confident that those hurdles will be overcome within a matter of years. How many years is an open question, of course, but even the most pessimistic observers are in agreement that both retail and business trading are now taking off. Near-term projections for European business trade, even by conservative Forrester Research, is that it will approach $60 million in annual revenues within another two years. Manufacturing and wholesaling will lead this advance, with the early national stars being Germany and the United Kingdom.

In spite of the Asian financial crisis, Asia also promises to be a player in the "early majority" uptake of E-business capability. One illuminating example is Asian Sources On-Line.

Based in Hong Kong and owned by Asia's largest trade publisher, this company went online in October 1995 as an electronic link between Asian exporters and international importers. Revenues come from a fixed fee paid by suppliers for the right to publish their home pages at the Asian Sources site. On their home pages, exporters identify who and where they are, what they sell, what terms they offer, and any contact details that a buyer might need; the pages also link to electronic catalogs. Access to the service is free for importers.

The ease and fluidity that the electronic model has brought into this trade arena has boosted profits for thousands of Asian suppliers and made Asian Sources On-Line a phenomenal success. Its initial membership of two hundred has grown to over 7,000, and the site contains descriptions of more than 42,000 items, ranging from garden furniture to computer monitors. Working with a start-up investment of only $6 million, the company has doubled its revenues for the past two years, and is now looking at an annual gross of over $10 million.

There are two important lessons to take away from this overnight success story.

First, in the world of the Web, *speed breeds speed.* It has been due entirely to the rapidity of Internet connections that Asian Sources On-Line has expanded its membership by an astonishing 3,500 percent in just three years. As one accolade puts it: "A manufacturer in a remote city in China can call Asian Sources in the morning; the company can take digital photos of their products and gather all the data about them in the afternoon; and Asian Sources On-Line can have this information on an importer's desk in New York, Frankfurt, or Sydney the following day."

The second lesson is that the *global market is wide open.* New York, Frankfurt, and Sydney, sure—but those are not the only places where Asian Sources has been successful. As counterintuitive as it may seem, a surprising amount of the company's early success has come from areas of the world that are technologically underdeveloped. For example, fewer than half of its users log on from North America, and there has been considerable interest from Latin America and Eastern Europe, where a savvy entrepreneur has a virtually open market, given the paucity of Net infrastructure already in place there. That goes double for Asian Sources's home base. They have worked very hard to alter the mind-set of traditional suppliers, to make Asians appreciate the potential of Internet commerce.

Obviously, they've been successful. And they're only one line of entry into a virtually unlimited market. For smaller businesses eventually, and larger businesses now, the computer-connected planet is becoming one market. In the era of the World Wide Web, the natural trajectory is away from the personal and toward the global.

The reason is that Internet connectivity is not just global, but *globalizing*. In following the law of plenitude, *it becomes its own growth engine*. The principle is perfectly illustrated by the story of PlanetAll, an Internet innovator that, by attacking the problem of disconnection on a very personal level, has in only two years become a global enabler.

PlanetAll Covers the World

The aptly named PlanetAll *(www.planetall.com)* provides its subscribers with access to what is surely the world's largest address book. Less than two years old, the Boston-based company boasts over 1.5 million members, and it was recently purchased by Amazon.com for over $100 million. It provides a good example not only of E-business's spectacular growth rate but also of the Internet's natural ability to globalize enterprises.

PlanetAll's president and cofounder, Warren Adams, explains that the idea for a Web-based address book goes back about ten years to his undergraduate days at Colgate University. Late one spring term, he started thinking about producing a directory that would enable friends who would be spending vacations in the same areas to keep in touch with one another over the summer.

> The idea was that people would give me their summer addresses and I would throw it all into a computer and print out a directory as well as personalized lists for individual locations. If you were going to be in Martha's Vineyard for the first week of August, then I could tell you, here are six other people that are going to be there at the same time that you wouldn't have known about otherwise.
>
> This was ten years ago, so it wasn't just pre-Internet, it was almost pre–PC, really the prehistoric era of contact management. We were just starting to go from typewriters to PCs. So at the time the concept would work only for a very isolated environment where you could have people come to your dorm room and put their schedules into your computer and you could then give them a print-out before the summer. It wasn't something that could be updated frequently. And it was definitely still in the "Wouldn't it be a good idea?" phase.
>
> The idea resurfaced six years later, when I was doing graduate work at Harvard Business School. Once again I was back in an environment where I was meeting all these people that I wanted to stay in touch with and losing touch with the people I had met during my five years of work prior to business school. Again the idea just sat there, and I left Boston and moved to London, where I went to work as a management consultant. It

wasn't until six months later that the address directory idea really started to jell.

What got it off the ground was my traveling from London to a college reunion in upstate New York. That weekend, I must have had fifteen people come up to me and say, "Gee, I wish I had known that you were in London. I was just there a week ago" or "I was there last month," and so on. That weekend pushed me over the edge. There was obviously such a need for a tool to help people stay in touch with the people they cared about.

This was two years ago. By that time, of course, the Web had taken off. The technology was there and the early adopters were using e-mail and it was starting to penetrate not just businesses but private homes. There are still hurdles out there, bandwidth wise and so on, for it to be ubiquitous. But we're definitely on the way, and PlanetAll is right at the head of the curve.

What makes PlanetAll's electronic product so different from traditional address books is the software-supported capacity for instant updating. Existing address books, whether they're print or electronic, become repositories of worthless information very quickly because of the rapid pace of life today. It's not just that you're constantly meeting more people, Adams explains, but that each of those new contacts has multiple "data points."

Everyone has an e-mail address now, and a cell phone, and probably a fax machine in his home as well as the office. So the task of staying in touch with 100 or 500 or a thousand people, especially as they move around, is becoming increasingly difficult. Our goal is to serve as the behind the scenes data infrastructure that keeps all this information up to date and makes it accessible to users no matter where they are and no matter what time it is.

Under the old paradigm of contact management, where you're constantly passing out business cards and manually entering changes in your electronic Rolodex, any time you change any small bit of information, you have to reach out to all those people—provided you even know how to reach them—and tell them, here's my new bit of information. At PlanetAll we've flipped that model on its head. We said, wouldn't it be easier if I just had to keep track of my *own* information and update that, and then decide who gets to see it and who doesn't?

Our software functions like an information switchboard, sending only the information you tell it to send to other individuals registered in the data base. Each user decides who should be informed of his birthday, a new job, or other information. You make all these individualized decisions at one entry point—your own hand held or desktop computer—and the information is propagated throughout the system, automatically updating the Web-based contact managers of every contact whom you've designated for the new information.

This is a tremendous timesaver for on-the-run professionals, and the gain is not just limited to personal contacts. Through the PlanetAll registry, you can also inform everybody from banks to subscription services when you move. College alumni organizations have shown a particular interest in the service, Adams notes, because it provides a more efficient way of keeping tabs on wandering graduates.

The system will tell your credit card companies, your frequent flyer services, your catalogues, your magazines, and pretty much anyone and any institution that you would need to tell when you make a change of address. It will even tell the post office so you don't have to go down and get a change of address form. There's still paperwork involved informing the postal authorities and magazines, but the third party partner who handles our fulfillment will eventually make that electronic too.

What started as a directory for college friends, then, has become a broad and flexible tool for international scheduling.

And all of this has happened in two short years. That's one of the amazing, although typical, features of many Web-based startups—the speed with which a new business model can take off. In PlanetAll's case, the principal metric used to track the expansion is membership numbers, and since January 1997, two months after the site was launched, those numbers have gone from 7000 to over 1.5 million.

That huge customer base is actually a composite, made up of two overlapping subsets. "We're really a couple of types of business," Adams says, "because we provide the service both to end users and to large organizations."

The end users are all the millions of individuals who want to be kept in touch with their myriad contacts. Those are our main customers, and what they get through the service is basically content. They're getting Joe's latest phone number and the fact that he just changed jobs and is now working in Denver for such and such a company. Joe is one of our end users, too, and he's actually the one who is providing the content that is making the product useful to all the other PlanetAll users who know him. In that sense our end use customers are also our suppliers.

The other subset of customers is the large organizations or

other Web sites who private label our technology. This isn't unique with us. Barnes & Noble was one of Firefly's big customers. Similarly, Lycos and GeoCities are our customers, and of course they have their own end users, whom we may acquire by acquiring the organization. The same is true of the many smaller organizations—alumni groups, industry associations, interest groups—who utilize us to help them keep track of their members. We've got over 80,000 group lists, and we're still growing.

This hybrid customer base enables PlanetAll to utilize a version of the "giveaway" strategy that was mentioned as an Internet pattern in Chapter 3. For end-use customers, the address book is free. "We make our money," Adams says, "by charging not the end user but our other customers and Web partners."

> We'll be moving soon to charging end users for certain features—like the updating of magazine subscriptions—but our model is to offer the basic service for free, and to generate revenue by licensing of the technology. It's a kind of "Intel inside" strategy. Lycos can offer our service as a contact management feature on its site, and either manage it on its own server or let us manage it for them. So we're positioned as part of their product, not as a stand-alone destination site.

The technical difficulty of managing PlanetAll's escalating database is a continuing challenge. Late in 1998, the company switched from its original server to a new platform with the capacity to satisfy literally tens of millions of users. In a traditional business, such numbers might be seen as overly optimistic. In a cyber universe that contains tens of millions of *current* Internet users, it's not an unreasonable projection of future growth.

The fundamental reason for that growth, Adams explains, is implicit in the business model itself, where the natural tendency of current users is to expand the service, telling other people about it so that they also can participate. Recall the law of plenitude that we mentioned in the Introduction. Adams sees a similar principle at work in PlanetAll's success.

The technical term is "network externality." We've seen it at work with the phone systems and the adoption of fax machines and, more recently, with the emergence of "buddy lists" on the Internet. Those are the lists that tell you in real time which of your friends is logged on at the same time you are, so you can zap them a good morning message. They've taken off phenomenally in the last two years, because it's users telling other potential users about the product—a kind of good-news virus spreading, on its own momentum.

We've been benefiting from the same kind of momentum, and this was something that was obvious right from the beginning. I remember sitting down two years ago with Michael Porter, one of my business school professors, and showing him an early Power Point presentation. He's renowned for strategy and competitive analysis, and when we got to this network externality effect, his eyes just lit up. "Wow," he said. "Your marketing's going to be done by the people actually using the product."

And that's exactly what happened. We went out at first to about 100 universities and had a rep at each of those campuses that got 50 or 100 people to sign up. Those first 50 or 100 were hard. But then we just walked away and let the virus spread. It happened at Harvard Business School and at MIT, and now the same thing is happening within companies. You get enough McKinsey consultants to sign up—it could be twenty or fifty—and they start telling the people that sit next to them and it just spreads throughout that organization.

We watch this growth group by group, and we think we're at a kind of threshold now, where we're having to consider whether it will take off more or whether we need to provide incentives to push it further. We've got our Planet Points Program that rewards you with points you can exchange for frequent flyer miles or charity donations or T-shirts and so on. But the first two years of our expansion was network externality.

The company's recent acquisition by Amazon.com, with its millions of customers, will connect the Boston-based firm to an even wider network. That acquisition was also an index of a broader strategy, by which the scheduling feature of the PlanetAll product line could enhance the bookseller's capacity to offer "frictionless shopping." That capacity, indeed, was the impetus for the two companies coming together in the first place. In the initial contacts, acquisition wasn't even on the drawing board. Adams explains:

That really came about without our seeking it. When we approached them in the summer of 1998, it wasn't at all about our being acquired. What we said was, you guys are all about e-commerce, and your business is about taking the friction out of shopping. That's why you brought it to the Web and you make it really easy. Well, a couple of other things can reduce the friction even more, and that's what we can bring to the table.

One is to let people know that there's an event in someone's life that warrants a purchase. Someone moves, somebody's birthday or anniversary is coming up, someone graduated, someone's coming to town—all of these events might prompt a purchase. A large number of the books and CDs and videos and whatever else Amazon's going to get into are already purchased as gifts for other people. Our ability to send reminders about those events was one element that made the integration look so logical.

Secondly, when you make that purchase, you need to know where to ship it. If your address book is right there, accessible on the same site, and you can just click on Joe's name with a birthday icon by it and it automatically gives you his up-to-date address, that's another level where you've reduced the friction.

Those were the two core reasons that integrating with Amazon made sense for us both. The comfort level was good, because they were willing to keep us in Boston under our own name, and obviously the valuation was right at the time as well. We've got a white board of ideas about where to go from here, but basically it's all about shopping and making the shopping experience easier for the consumer.

If this sounds like Business 101, that shouldn't be surprising. Like most E-business pioneers, Adams is intently focused on basic business principles, in building value for his customers and for potential investors. When he speaks about opportunities on the Web, it's in very traditional terms. For all the flurry about technology, he insists, a company's relationship to its customers is still the decisive factor in any business.

One of the biggest things that Web-based business has done is to give us better, quicker information about customers, and that helps us to understand the lifetime value of a customer. The web gives you so much more data to measure that value and assess it. So you know exactly what your cost of acquisition is.

You also have detailed knowledge of customer behavior. Not just at the purchase point, either. As long as there have been credit cards, you've been able to determine how many books someone buys at Barnes & Noble. By tracking traffic on a Web site, you can go way beyond that. You can identify not just individual purchases but also purchasing patterns and even the steps of a customer's decision process. You can tell how he's walking around the electronic store because you know he clicked on Tom Clancy before he went off and bought Danielle Steel. So, that's one thing that's changed.

But a lot of other things, Adams says, have not really changed. Not, at least, in ways that affect core competencies, that have an impact on the long-term success of a company, or that have an influence on stock valuation. Internet pioneers like Amazon.com, for example, are frequently taken to task for not yet making a profit—and the implication, among analysts who emphasize this point, is that the soaring Wall Street rates that they are enjoying are blatantly inconsistent with their red-ink position. Adams takes a longer, more auspicious view:

> People say, these companies aren't spinning off a lot of cash yet. How can they be worth anything? But think back to the early years of cable, when there was a lot of investment in marketing and product development before anybody ever saw decent returns. It was the same with pharmaceuticals. There was a lot of money spent on developing Viagra before a penny was earned

on it. That's the way up-front investment works, maybe always has worked.

It would be interesting to go back into business history and look at the early oil industry, when wildcatters were going out and purchasing real estate in desolate areas where there *might* be oil. They paid for that real estate, sometimes on nothing more than a hunch, and it got more and more expensive and eventually a few of them struck oil, so that the investment did yield a profit, but not right away.

After that, of course, the major players like Standard Oil moved in and bought up the best real estate and consolidated. I think we'll see something very similar in Internet industries. I look at the Yahoos and Amazons as the Standard Oils of the new world, and they're buying up the small to mid-size players now. The "long shot" of oil became the basis of an entire economy in the 19th century. I'm confident that the Internet will play a similar role. It will be in everybody's lives and become the common standard for how people everywhere do business. So if you think that Amazon.com or any of these other big players are overvalued, remember that history.

Adams brings the same sanguine view to his own company's success. Meteoric as that has been, he is very aware that building a base is a long-haul proposition. That conviction underlies PlanetAll's free sign-up policy as well as its desire to partner with the cyberspace's Standard Oils—to make itself visible via Lycos and Amazon.com. "The business design," Adams says, "is to make this thing ubiquitous."

Remember Eric Schmidt's witty definition of URL: "Ubiquity now, Revenue Later." It's an insight that the PlanetAll story dramatically illustrates. Although, given network externality, it may be sooner rather than later.

Making Entertainment Pay

In stressing the evolution of the Net toward globalizing business, we do not mean to deny the continued attraction of the medium as a vehicle for more purely entertaining activities. But these activities, too, in the logic of the Net, will become either commerce savvy or increasingly private and invisible.

A recent Forrester Research report on Internet games, for example, documented the slow initial growth of online gaming but predicted that, once the disparate activity of current gaming becomes consolidated in "game centers," we may expect a tripling of revenues in this segment over the next couple of years. Currently, this form of online entertainment is hindered by bandwidth and "latency" issues—the latter referring to the slow delivery of game instructions to online players—as well as by the lack of a clear and consistent business model and the fact that the segment's core market, young males, is "awash in console-based and CD-ROM games." Online game centers, say the report's authors, "will clear away the technology, customer acquisition, and business model underbrush that hold this market back," so that annual revenues may surpass $1.6 million early in the new century.

If they're right, once that occurs, we'll see at least this form of Net-based entertainment follow the same commerce-intensive path as so many other industries. Following the lead of Microsoft's Internet Gaming Zone and other early entrants, game centers will establish commerce systems with integrated payment options and online storefronts; form partnerships with third-party authorization firms like CyberCash; and reach beyond their core market to more sedate and broader audiences—chess players, for example. And they will follow the lead of PlanetAll and other free-subscription services by garnering revenue from on-site advertising and sponsorships.

One of the more interesting spin-offs of this trend will be a blurring of the customer-perceived boundary between games and ads, as sponsors' spots are embedded in the game design itself. "Companies like Nike, Spalding, and Gatorade," say the report's sponsors, "can reach their on-line clientele more effectively if they partner with Yoyodyne Entertainment or Sandbox Entertainment to sponsor on-line sports leagues."

This is a strategy that we mentioned in the last chapter, with the example of the Fastball-Gap partnership, and it's one that is entirely consistent with the direction of the Net. It's not that entertainment will be simply overshadowed by business, but that the entertainment which dominates will be business-driven. Like everything else in this fundamentally commerce-driven medium, infotainment will be not so much bypassed as absorbed.

Rules and No Rules

Joe Lassiter, Professor of Management at Harvard Business School and the former president of Wildfire Communications, has researched dozens of Internet start-up companies. In his view, rather than there being a conflict between the Net-as-entertainment-complex and the Net-as-global-enterprise-zone, there's a kind of creative tension between the two images. "You can think of the Net," he says, "as similar to the old American West."

It was important in that era to have some legal right-of-ways established, where the railroads could push forward and open the space up for settlement. But it was also important, in a lot of places, to have no rules. That was part of the attraction—the risk and the fluidity in a space where you also had an emerging governmental stability.

The really interesting thing about the Web today is that, instead of a government having to build the whole "track," everybody gets to build little pieces of it. Everybody is experimenting with his own rules, and sometimes—with a company like Cisco, for example—the innovation actually becomes the rules—or the standards—by which the Web will be built. What all this diverse activity means is that, intellectually and economically, the innovator can proceed at a remarkably rapid pace, and this creates a great atmosphere of innovation. Periodically it gets out of control—that happened in the West, too—but there's a whole tension evolving between rules and no-rules, and ultimately that kind of tension is essential for rapid progress.

Of course, harnessing the tension can be a tricky business. As the next chapter will indicate, Professor Lassiter's Old West analogy has an even broader relevance to the Net's "wide open spaces" than is indicated here, because some of the most dynamic challenges in this arena—both in terms of rules and of innovation—are being posed by the medium's earliest "pioneers."

Chapter 5

Internet Pioneers Will Reshape Their Industries

Although the "E" in E-business stands for "electronic," it could just as well stand for experimentation. If there is one feature that distinguishes Internet businesses from their traditional counterparts, that feature is the willingness to reconstruct patterns. Today's E-business pioneers are doing what the great pioneers of the past—the Edisons, the Fords, the Gutenbergs—have always done: sized up the tried-and-true methods of playing the game and said to themselves, impatiently, "Let's try something *new.*"

If you want to make it in this space, forget what you "know." Start with the premise that premises, as a (cyber) rule, may be wrong. Look, for example, at the Web's single most amazing retail success story: that of the self-styled "largest bookstore in the world."

Invisible Inventory

Amazon.com is an electronic bookseller headquartered in Seattle. The founders placed their company in Pioneer Square, a quaint section of downtown that has been restored to its original gaslight-era elegance. This bookseller built a reputation by offering more titles than any other store in the world; it claims to offer more than three million titles online. The difference between shopping here and at another bookstore down the street is that you will never enter a physical door to a roomful of bookshelves. The only doors open to you are virtual portals to a virtual company that offers a huge collection of virtual titles.

Why virtual titles? Because when you get online, you see no stacks, and you can't pick up a book and read its jacket or turn a few pages to measure the quality of the work. You can't heft it in your hand or feel its texture with a loving finger. In fact, if you actually were allowed to wander around the physical rooms of this electronic store, you would very likely be unimpressed.

First, you wouldn't see three million books. If you were lucky, and a bit patient, you might actually see where several hundred were stored in boxes on shelves, or see some lying around to be entered into Amazon's online database. Amazon.com's enormous inventory of books, a number that rivals the capacity of major libraries, is virtual, too. It exists as a potential, a digital possibility that is made real, made physical, only by a customer's decision to buy a particular book. This decision triggers an avalanche of electronic operations, including a command to send a book to the customer's address from a physical inventory somewhere on the planet and a corresponding e-mail message confirming the shipment.

"Somewhere" actually means "many places," for Amazon.com's massive inventory, practically invisible in Seattle, is actually housed physically in other booksellers' and publishers' warehouses, available to the company (and its customers) at the click of a mouse. "Invisible," therefore, may be a little overstated. It's really a *distributed* inventory—a business concept that has underlain just-in-time manufacturing for decades, and that the Seattle entrepreneurs have modified brilliantly.

For customers, of course, "distributed" and "invisible" are immaterial. It doesn't matter to them where a book is sent from, as long as it arrives at their doorstep promptly. With Amazon.com's rapid delivery service—many books are shipped within twenty-four hours—that concern is also covered automatically.

Because the company is online, and highly computerized throughout, they can also offer features that you won't find in most bookstores. These include a weekly list compiled by its editors that profiles bestsellers as well as up-and-comers; competitive discounts that range from 10 to 40 percent on books listed in the *New York Times Book Review;* and a recommendation center that gives repeat visitors specific suggestions based on their previously demonstrated interests, their favorite authors, books they have liked or disliked, and their past purchases from Amazon. This last service, which relies on cookie technology, provides the personalized attention that is increasingly important in cyberspace.

Amazon.com is a public company, following a very successful initial public offering in May 1997. In the process of preparing for this offering, they raised the ire of traditional booksellers who viewed them as a potential killer competitor. In attempting to derail the offering, Barnes & Noble, a well-respected "traditional" bookseller, sued the potential start-up over its claim that it was able to offer (at that time) over two million titles. Barnes & Noble literally dared Amazon to compare the number of books they had on their premises with the large number of titles that the bookseller had on the shelves of a typical store.

Not only was this a tempest in a teapot; it was based on false premises. From the way they approached the Seattle challenge, it was clear that Barnes & Noble had misunderstood the dynamics of a new marketing model, especially with regard to the delivery of commodity items. In good nineteenth-century fashion, they envisioned their business as a *place* containing physical items. If a certain item wasn't already in that place, their strategy—and they were proud of it—was to order the item, that is, to bring it to the place, and then to ask that the customer come and take it to his or her place. A bookstore, thus, was seen as a switching depot, an essential intermediary between publisher and customer.

Only it wasn't essential. That's what Amazon.com has proved. And, although Barnes & Noble honestly believed that Amazon.com was misrepresenting itself to consumers, the truth was actually a little more subtle—and more significant. The point which Amazon.com has made eloquently is that virtual companies are different from "traditional companies." Virtual companies don't need large on-site inventories. In fact, they don't want large inventories. They want *zero* inventories on-site, and instant access to distributed inventories elsewhere. That's what makes virtual selling work. It's what makes just-in-time manufacturing work. And it's what Amazon.com taught the entire book industry.

Its initial confusion aside, Barnes & Noble by now has got the picture, and it has now repositioned itself to become

Amazon.com's chief online competitor. Its print ads boast of a database over 50 percent larger than Amazon.com's, and its Web site may be even better than Amazon.com's in providing that sense of community that book lovers crave: After all, B&N pioneered the once radical concept of turning its bookstores into cafés with books on the side. The struggle for preeminence in this space is bound to go on.

Amazon.com has been a true phenomenon, but it's not unique. There are many other pioneers that are profiting from the virtual marketplace, and that have been able to see, in this first five years, the real possibilities that the Internet can provide business innovators. Here are examples from three of the hottest online areas: travel, music, and computers.

Tickets Plus

Travel-related sales is the single biggest online selling category, and San Francisco–based Preview Travel is a pioneer in this lucrative field. Beginning as a travel videotape producer in the mid-1980s, Preview entered cyberspace in 1994, offering airline bookings online; today it has branched into the related fields of car rental and hotel reservations, and it also offers its own vacation deals.

Its success has been rapid and remarkable. Staff has gone from five to nearly two hundred—three quarters of whom work in online operations. The online "offices," supported by an exclusive partnership with America Online, average about 125,000 hits a day. Bookings have been growing at a rate of nearly 300 percent a year and, although the company is not expected to turn a profit until the year 2000, its online commission takes have also been soaring. They are currently the Internet's number-one travel provider. Preview Travel's success is testimony to the power of virtuality, and it illustrates a number of basic principles about doing business online.

First is the wisdom—many analysts call it a necessity—of supporting an infant operation with sufficient *capital backing.* Second is the value of *strategic alliances;* here the $32 million that Preview paid AOL has proved a wise investment in resulting online traffic. "The exclusivity and the number of impressions we get fuels the business," says Preview president and CEO Ken Orton. Last but certainly not least is the importance of remembering that, online no less than off-line, *convenience* is key. Speaking of a recent joint project with the travel book publisher Fodor's (the partnership principle again), Orton enthuses about his company's ability to integrate Fodor's book content with Preview's multimedia capabilities and reservation service, so that "we're providing the content necessary for people to do all the research and all the buying in one fell swoop." Preview is moving, therefore, toward one-stop shopping—something that today's frequent fliers consider a premium worth paying for.

What are the bottom-line lessons of Preview's success? James Oliver Cury, who interviewed Orton for a Texas computer magazine, sums it up well. Preview, he writes, took "all the steps that cyber pundits recommend. It sought growth capital from investors, expanded its horizons beyond reservations by offering its own brand of vacation packages, exploited the Web medium, partnered with Fodor's to provide online travel guides, marketed the heck out of the site, and always remembered that the customer comes first." It's perfectly predictable that, given this first-mover example, the aging lions of the travel world have followed suit. Among the options now offered by many of the major airlines is the simplified online booking that Preview pioneered.

Music on the Net

One of the fastest growing product and purchasing categories on the Internet is music. And the phenomenal interest in online music is boosting E-business as well, accounting for sales levels of nearly $50 million a year. One reason for this impressive growth is that people have found the Internet to be a perfect medium for music, and the multimedia PC the perfect Net instrument. In sharp contrast to Internet video, which loses significant quality on its transmission along the Internet, streaming audio, a technique used to send sound over the Internet, allows music to be played at high quality on the speakers that may accompany today's desktop computers. As a result, major players in the music industry are positioning themselves to cash in on this expanding segment. A few indicators:

- Record labels, from Atlantic to Warner Bros., are increasingly creating their own Net presences, showcasing their offerings through custom Web sites.
- The teenage channel surfer's port of first call, MTV, has teamed with a major search engine, Yahoo!, to provide customized search capability for music sites, events, and reviews.
- One Intel-sponsored event, the New York Music Festival in the summer of 1997, Web-cast the performances of over 400 bands around the world live.

Prominent in this space is another Yahoo! partner, CDNow, which, with its menu of over 250,000 music-oriented products, is one of the largest online music sellers. Founded in 1994 by brothers Jason and Mathew Olim in their parents' basement, CDNow currently boasts a 200,000-plus customer base and controls 33 percent of the online retail music market, twice as large a share as its closest rival. They have built their success not only on their extensive inventory, but also on providing value added features that go beyond sales.

For example, site visitors can download song ratings and reviews; comb listings of concert dates, the week's hot singles, and biographies of prominent artists; and utilize the CDNow search engine to check the availability of obscure releases. In addition, as in any good electronic meeting place, CDNow offers a chat line for fans to share their thoughts on the latest release or concert.

CDNow also leverages the real-time delivery of product previews. Its customers can not only electronically browse from among 100,000 CD and cassette titles, but can preview them online, listening to a track before they buy. This is not just an equivalent experience to visiting a music store—most people who use CDNow consider it a better one, because you don't have to spend the time going to a "real" music store, only to discover that its selection is more limited than CDNow's. Here is one example where the "texture" of the digital experience is actually richer than that of the physical equivalent.

The sound delivery capability of the Internet hasn't so much built a new music business as it has created a new, Net-based music community, with a growing number of dedicated listeners who depend on the Web for much of their music. Live events, especially those that were not available through television, can now be accessed at home through the Internet along with other visual and text information. Such musical Web-cast experiences are shared experiences, in that each listener knows that he is part of a real-time community. That's a significant lesson: One common feature of successful Web sites is that they leverage commonality of interests, or "affinity."

Order Checks and Spouse Checks

If travel is the major moneymaking service online, the product leader, hands-down, is computers. Given the nature of the Internet, this is not surprising. Yet because business journalists tend to focus on offerings such as flights to Aruba, the latest Garth Brooks CD, and pornography, the dominance of computers in E-business is sometimes forgotten. Only avid cybersales watchers are aware that about *half* of all online revenues are generated from computers or from computer-related products like software and computer-related books. Or that, of the Web sites chosen by *Net Marketing* magazine as the Top 200 business-to-business sites of 1997, fully one third belonged to computer firms.

One leader in this field is Dell Computers. Building on its success in mail-order PC sales, the Texas company is gradually migrating to the Net, and expects to do half of its business there by the turn of the century. Its site already pulls in $4 million of revenue every day, from the literally tens of millions of potential shoppers who visit every year.

What makes Dell stand out is a fusion of customized ordering, follow-up service, and constant refinement. To facilitate customization, the company employs a modular online sales tool so

that its customers can build infinitely personalized system packages. To enhance postorder service, Dell allows them to follow up
on their orders with an option called Order Watch, which in-
forms them, via e-mail, when their order was shipped, and with
what carrier. (FedEx and UPS offer similar tracking services.) As
for refinement, the company runs frequent "usability" studies, to
ensure that the Web site's intended functions are being fully realized. In some of these studies, the company directly polls its Web
site visitors ("What do you think this feature means?") and tabu-
lates the results. Other "studies," as Dell Online senior manager
Bill Morris explains, are less formalized.

> A lot of our studies are what we internally call spouse checks.
> You take it home and say, "Whaddaya think?" What we found
> out is that spouse checks tend to track very closely with usabil-
> ity studies. I found out that my wife can think just like Fortune
> 500 IS managers from a usability standpoint. The point is to do
> everything you can to get another set of eyeballs on the changes
> you're proposing, because what's very apparent to you and your
> colleagues may not be as intuitive as you thought.

That's a basic lesson of doing business on the Internet. No
matter how high-tech you get, it's still about customers. Technology drives E-business, but it's not *about* technology. It's about *using* technology to empower yourselves and your customers.

Transformed Industries? Mixed Results

One thing that all these stories have in common is that they highlight the premium that the Internet places on aggressive entry—on what analysts frequently refer to as the first mover advantage. But that fact in itself is less useful than merely interesting. Success stories are seldom important in and of themselves, after all; if they were, we'd still be discussing the hula hoop phenomenon. The ultimate value of a success story lies in its impact, and it's here that we can see the real importance of these celebrated cases. Their broader, social implications may be in paradigm rattling, that is, in the way that their novel approaches to their respective industries have already rewritten the rules under which those industries operate.

Harvard Business School management professor Joe Lassiter, whose area of expertise is the sales and marketing efforts of start-ups and buyouts, reflected on this point in a recent conversation. According to Professor Lassiter, the broader lesson of the Amazon.com case—and not just for the book industry—is that the Internet makes it possible to take a classic business challenge, the management of inventory, and essentially turn it on its head.

> Amazon has truly transformed that business. There is a financial model that you use to generate the cash flow characteristics of a business, and in the end, all the hype aside, cash flow is what drives any business. The elements of cash flow are growth rate, profitability, and asset intensity. And asset intensity, which is where the inventory issue comes in, relates to how

many dollars you have to have in place to run the business. Well, Amazon's got a business model that *doesn't require plant*. Beyond that, it doesn't take inventory, yet you and I pay up front when we order a book. This means that it has, literally, negative asset intensity. In other words, the faster it grows, the more cash it can throw off to finance its growth.

The model is so attractive that other big booksellers have had to react, copying the model and trying to drive the Amazon competitive advantage down. But fundamentally these other stores, the Barnes & Nobles and Borders, have got what in this space is an archaic business model for a large part of their business, because their existing view of the world requires physical stores to house and display the physical inventory. While some customers will always demand touching the merchandise, a lot of customers—and investors—will find themselves better served by the Amazon-type experience. Everybody at Borders and Barnes & Noble is hunting for ways to radically reform their business models in response to the Amazon innovation.

As competitors copy Amazon's model, Amazon's value will decrease because the alternatives will compete, prices will be driven down, and the premium of the original innovation will disappear. Amazon knows that, which is why they are betting that they can take advantage of the Internet to be more than a network efficiencies type business, growing to provide more links to other services. Other services will link back to them faster than their competitors can duplicate, and so the value of the combined services and the virtual user community will enhance Amazon's competitive advantage. People go to the Amazon site not just to buy books, but to read the book reviews that they can't find anywhere else, to visit chat rooms that originate there, to accumulate frequent shopper discounts, and so on.

This has a very distinctive effect on, among other things, my own ordering for the course I teach. I have to put together a reading list every year for my students. I can put together a better reading list faster on Amazon.com than I can with the proprietary tools that are available anywhere else. In addition, my students avoid bookstore lines, and if they decide to buy a supplemental book, they click on it and it's shipped to them tomorrow. The convenience factor here is just unbelievable. Of course, Barnes & Noble is copying, and probably even innovating on, the Amazon model.

But this visible impact of the Web as a whole on an industry, Lassiter points out, is still the exception rather than the rule. There's a wide array of responses to such first-mover gambits, ranging from instant replication to sluggish disinterest. Another Internet pioneer, for example, has been the online car dealer Autobytel.com, about which we'll say more in the following chapter. The automobile industry's reaction to this innovation, he says, demonstrates that not all innovations are universally copied.

The book industry, slow as it might sometimes appear, has actually responded quicker than many other industries. In terms of the big stories of Internet success, you've seen a relatively fast reaction in the book industry by competitors like Barnes & Noble, a slower one within the travel industry, and an even slower one in the automotive industry. And within that industry, it goes exactly how you think it would go. The big players are moving pretty slowly, while the small players are challenging the whole way cars are sold and the way car salespeople relate to customers.

If there's a pattern here, Lassiter says, it may have to do with the age and related agility of the business. The older players, like GM, just seem less responsive when it comes to "reforming" their traditional ways of doing things.

> There's a leader interested in reforming nearly every business today, and the Internet is the tool of choice for doing that. Amazon is one leader. Virtual Vineyards is another. There are new category entrants like AllHerb in the homeopathic drug business. There's Chemdex in the specialty chemical business. And very often, where you find success in transforming existing businesses, you find that the reforming is being done by start-ups or buyouts that are forced by the constraints of capital and time to innovate, or fail.
>
> This isn't just funky start-up corporate culture, it's people. The old companies find it difficult to keep the Net-savvy people, the exciting people, with them. They go to the new companies, the ones that are already Internet enabled. It happens in California and in Boston more than in any other places, because that's where you find an infrastructure of human beings and money and expertise that encourages all this new, experimental activity.

Since Boston and California have long been geographical hot spots for the personal computer industry, it's not surprising that Professor Lassiter is enthusiastic about that industry. Interestingly, though, one of the major players in that space—and a prime example of a paradigm-rattling pioneer—is headquartered midway between them, in Austin, Texas. Lassiter is very impressed with the first-mover contributions of Dell Computer.

At this point Dell is tearing up the NASDAQ board, and no-body thinks there's a secret to how they did it. The great thing about Dell is that the customer can service himself, and he tends to buy more than he would if he had a salesperson in the middle. With the online model, you get risk-averse shopping, lots of high-end buys—maybe overbuys, maybe just safe buys—and Dell doesn't even have to pay the salesperson for upselling.

Dell actually started selling on the phone years ago, and the move to the Web was simply a logical extension of the strategy, because it gives both Dell and the customer greater speed and lower cost. And the model is inevitably transforming the PC industry. Eventually, everybody is going to be designing—liter-ally "configuring"—his or her computer from home, because the Dell model will be universally adopted. It has to be. It's the attraction of negative asset intensity that you can't ignore.

But it's not quite "absolutely automatic" yet, and that's an impor-tant point. You can buy and configure a Dell computer online, but you can also still talk to the phone representative, walk into any one of a thousand Dell resellers, or even buy a refurbished PC from the Dell warehouse outlet. Even this Internet leader still uses a mixture of channels. We'll learn more about mixtures like this in the following chapter.

Chapter 6

Market Models Will Multiply, Not Contract

The rush to the Web in recent years has been so tremendous that to some observers it seems like a universal juggernaut, destined to be nothing less than the Single Wave of the Future. As Eric Schmidt, chairman and CEO of Novell, points out, there is a certain madcap rationale to this common perception, although it's based less on clear strategic thinking than on frenzied reaction. What we're seeing, Eric suggests, is a "kind of mass hysteria."

Normally, you wouldn't have people spending millions and millions of dollars to enter new channels without a reasonably high expectation of return. But in this climate, where nobody wants to be left behind, people are throwing away any kind of rational business analysis and spending money aimlessly just to say "We're on line." The only people who are really profiting from that attitude are the 22 year olds who are designing Web sites.

Of course there's some point to the hysteria, because in a market that is growing as rapidly as the Internet market, very small differences in timing can equate to huge differences in market share. The term that's used in the industry is called *first mover advantage*. If you look at start-ups generally, not just Web start-ups, there's an enormous advantage to being the first to enter a market. When you do that, you get to define the market, and everybody else has to position against you.

But this isn't new. It's an old, timeless business principle. You get in first, gain customers, lock them in, and make them happy. The difference is in the speed with which that can happen today, and the speed with which an early presence can translate into perceived market share. The Internet paradigm is a rapid, interactive one. And that interactivity leads to reactivity.

But does this mean that the Internet becomes the dominating channel? Or the only channel? That more traditional channels will be simply swamped, and that within a matter of years, as some have predicted, all commercial activity will be conducted, by forfeit, on the Web?

Variety of Usage Patterns

Not in our estimation—or in Eric's. If you begin by considering only the variety of usage patterns, Eric says, "we're not even getting close yet to Web-only purchasing."

There is a small set of people who buy virtually everything over the Web. I can certainly understand them, because I'm one of them. Whatever I'm buying, I start by looking first on the Net. I bought an airplane over the Net. It was delivered in physical space, and I had to go and visit the airplane just to make sure it was really there, but the purchasing process and documentation all happened electronically. But that's an anomaly, obviously. Most people's Web shopping is much less elaborate, less extensive, than that.

But they may use the Web quite extensively as a consumer research tool. Even if they don't end up buying there, they know that the Web really specializes in dispensing information, and I think it's even reasonable to assert that the market in general can become more efficient if more people consulted the Web first for accurate information.

For example, I bought a camera recently, a special mid-format camera, not a 35-millimeter one, and I didn't know what I was doing. In this case I didn't use the Web. I went to a camera store, and they told me which one to buy. OK, I got it home, eventually figured it out, looked at the pictures. I was pretty satisfied, but then I got on the Web, and I found out there that this camera required a very specific lens for high-contrast work. This was well known to all the photography buffs on the Web, but my salesman didn't know it.

How would my shopping experience have changed if I had known that ahead of time? Maybe very little, maybe a lot. I doubt that I would have bought this particular camera directly from the Web. I needed to talk to somebody in person, even if that person wasn't particularly well-informed. But at least I would have had that extra information, and that's one of the two things that the Web is really good for. It's either an origination mechanism or it's a source of ongoing information and product upgrades. I use it for both those things, but other people use it only for information.

Beyond "One Size Fits All"

In addition to these differences in user patterns, Eric points out, there are also differences in product and service configurations that make the transference of *everything* to the Net an unlikely prospect. Is there a natural trajectory toward monopoly on the Net? Or are there certain purchases—like Eric's camera—that require, for whatever reason, a human interaction? Eric is not ready yet to count out off-line channels:

What percentage of goods do you think you'll buy on the Net in the next year? Let's say 10 percent. Ninety percent you'll buy in physical space. And that 10 percent, if you fit the usual pattern, are going to be computer-related items, a few commodities like books and music, and information services like stock trading. Over time, you'll increase your percentage as more goods become available on the Net, and what you'll discover as you do that is that *if you know what you want,* the Net is the most efficient way to get it. If you don't know what you want, it's just about the worst place to get it, because there's no editor.

So, what if there *was* an editor—a huge store directory—for any kind of purchase you wanted to make? Why couldn't a smart capitalist build a store—let's call it the Everything Store—which had every single item for sale in the world, and that also had my credit card, my profile, all my interests and preferences? Then I could just log on, make a data connection, type in the name of what I wanted, press a button, and it would show up tomorrow on my doorstep. This could happen, this huge, all-encompassing, electronic version of Kmart or Wal-Mart.

Is it likely? I don't know. Before the Internet came along, with its vastly distributed inventories, we never had the capability of having a store with everything in the world in it. It's technically feasible. But there are limitations, human limitations and therefore marketing limitations.

For me, when I'm buying books, the only time I go to a bookstore is when I don't know what I'm looking for. But that's not true of everybody. Plenty of people want that Starbucks and the padded armchair experience. Or they want to talk to their banker face to face—even though local banking is something that the Internet could easily eliminate. Or they want local service. You may continue to buy your TV from a local distributor in case it breaks.

So, there's a distinction here that we don't yet know how to verbalize. It appears as though a few sets of things will become massive monopoly stores because of convenience—books may be one example, banking and financial services may be another. And in networks, cost economies definitely favor the global player. On the other hand, even I walk into a camera store. And I still look at magazine ads, to get further information. So it's definitely not all one channel, and it's not one-size-fits-all.

Concurring with Eric's assessment is John White, the former chief information officer of the computer giant Compaq. John sees the Web not as closing off previous marketing possibilities but as a fluid arena that encourages different corporate "personalities." For example, to those who wonder whether the "real" Web is an electronic Dodge City or a more private fief of cyberspace's business interests, he observes that these two models are not necessarily incompatible.

The flexibility of the Internet allows us to have both personalities equally well supported. The underlying technology offers the capability to distribute anything to anyone. Therefore, it can support an audience of open consumers, where anybody can get access to unprotected information, where it's visible and open to the public. And it can support an audience that's more concerned with security.

The Internet has the capability of supporting, in effect, a whole range of virtual private networks *inside* the major network. Every company that does commerce on line establishes an extended community of users with whom it's willing to share information about supply and demand requirements. You can set these virtual communities up and with the appropriate security control you can have either a closed community of interest or an open community running on the same infrastructure.

One of the business opportunities that I think is going to emerge soon is that certain businesses will want a high degree of security *and* a high degree of availability, of robustness—say a response time of 27 milliseconds for a particular function. And these companies are going to be willing to pay for this, because it's a business value for them to deliver that level of service.

If you are gaining access to an open, public, mutual trust network like the Internet was originally supposed to be, then you tolerate some pretty horrendous response times, and you don't complain much because you're getting the service, slow as it is, almost for free. But with a more closed, private system, you can demand better responses. That's why companies like AT&T and MCI-Worldcom are going to be able to run a profitable business by offering closed community access at higher service levels to the customers who demand that business advantage.

As we get better and better about these things and we have these high value points that bring the level of service and the level of functionality up, then we begin to commoditize that service level and everyone begins to enjoy it, to take it for granted. In addition, we may work through a mixture of virtual and physical networks. When you work exclusively over the Internet, it's so complex that you can't always know exactly where your data is going or what service provider is going to carry it. For that reason, I have been concerned about the Internet being able to stand up to the demands. It is such a unique example of shared provisioning.

So I think there may be some business functions that require that their networks are delivered over an AT&T provided facility or an MCI-Worldcom provided facility in order to ensure that they have the appropriate quality of service. For others, the Internet alone will be ideal. But there will continue to be different kinds of service and service levels.

Those service levels, as John's discussion indicates, are determined not by some ideal channel mix but by customer demand—demand that is related to purchasing patterns. Those patterns, subtly transformed by cyber rules, are tremendously varied, and nimble companies recognize and respond to this. That's why Wells Fargo Bank, which has a great interactive Web site, continues to maintain branches around the country. Why Intuit, maker of the popular financial-planning package Quicken, sells it both over the Net and at Office Depot. And why J. Crew, which started out as a traditional brick-and-mortar clothier, moved first to mail-order catalogs, then to the Net, and is now selling its merchandise in all three venues.

Opportunities on the Internet are so huge and they get realized so quickly that it's a very attractive place to put marginal dollars. But it's not, and never will be, the only place. Customers can't be pigeonholed into a single channel, and if you want to optimize sales, you've got to recognize that fact.

Consider, to drive the point home, the "prelimination" factor.

The "Prelimination" Factor

Eric Schmidt's personal pattern of nearly all-Web shopping is unusual. Only a small percentage of potential Internet customers actually end up making all of their purchases there. For many more—in the retail field, they are still a majority—shopping the

Web means gathering product information that they can use in making better informed purchasing decisions, which they may very well implement in a brick-and-mortar venue.

They use the search capabilities of the infinite market, in other words, to *preview* the available options in the physical market and then to *eliminate* those that don't conform to their tastes or their budget. They are engaging in an activity that might be called "prelimination." The open architecture of the Net, and its remarkable slice-and-dice capabilities, make it an ideal tool to encourage and help shape this activity. There's a marvelous opening here, as yet faintly realized.

Only a few businesses as of yet have adequately realized that *enhancing* your customer base's preliminating power—rather than nudging them, subtly, toward this quarter's overstock—might end up saving everybody both time and money. This is the "negative" version, if you will, of mass customization, and it may be an E-business model that is waiting to happen. For example, the filtering of possible matches that online middlemen now employ is really a type of prelimination on the customer's behalf. If you look at a keyword search in its broadest sense, you can see that Yahoo! and Excite are also "preliminating" services: They enable the customer to zero in on his most focused interests. And many retailers use their Web sites to steer people toward their stores, with the customers using those sites for preshopping filtering.

Channel Hybridity: Two Auto Sellers

Or consider the stories of two very different automobile sellers. The first, Autobytel.com, is widely known because, as Harvard

Business School's Joe Lassiter mentioned in the previous chapter, it has been a catalyst for change in certain segments of the auto industry.

Autobytel.com. Applying the lesson of Web-based fluidity has made this company one of the great success stories of the Net's first generation. Even though it stayed in the red for its first three years, it has emerged as the nation's premier online car dealer.

Wait a minute, conventional thinking would say. Doesn't the idea of buying an automobile sight unseen violate basic principles of intelligent shopping? Doesn't a purchase of this magnitude absolutely call for on-the-spot, kick-the-tires involvement? Because of channel hybridity, the answer is "Yes and No," or rather "Yes, No, and Sometimes."

Autobytel.com was started by California entrepreneur Peter Ellis, and the "break the rules" model that he introduced was no-haggle car buying. An "analog" car dealer until 1995, Ellis launched his company that year on the Prodigy service, and he set up as an independent Web site shortly thereafter. Since then, the virtual company has not only grown rapidly (doing $2 billion of business in its first year, and accounting for 1 percent of all new-car sales last year) but is also having a ripple effect on car sales in general. Chrysler estimated recently that it was doing between 1 percent and 2 percent of its worldwide sales through online services, and there is not a major car manufacturer that doesn't run a Web site. This isn't even counting the other auto "superstores"—AutoNation, AutoVantage, and CarMax—that have followed Ellis's model to online success.

That model is simple but powerful. Autobytel.com enrolls over

2,000 individual dealerships in its virtual superstore, keeps track of their inventories in a central database, and sends them leads based on buyers' queries to the Web site. The queries are free, but for the privilege of being listed in this extremely lucrative space, Ellis charges dealers an annual fee of $2,500, plus a monthly charge that's set on a sliding scale from $150 to $1,500, depending on how much (closed) business he sends their way.

Because Autobytel.com is a superstore representing a large number of clients from a single electronic storefront, it profits handily from economies of scope and of scale. Its leads, for example, cost the subscribing dealers only about twenty-five dollars each—far less than the hundreds of dollars that traditional sales methods, including advertising and promotion, require. Other advantages to the dealers are also dramatic. Their decreased overhead allows them to sell cars at rock-bottom prices and still turn a profit. It also significantly extends the selling range, allowing them to compete with other dealers that they would normally not even see. A New Jersey dealership that subscribes to the Autobytel.com service, for example, sells about fifty cars a month through the service, and considers each sale to be incremental business.

Analysts expect that by 2000, over 25 percent of car buyers will be shopping online. This will require significant growth of the online industry, but Autobytel.com is prepared. Autobytel.com expects to raise almost $60 million for future growth when they finally do their IPO. Their sales rose to $5 million last year, up from only one quarter million the year before.

But how do customers utilize Autobytel.com? Here is where the "Yes, No, and Sometimes" response comes in—and where we encounter a type of "channel hybridity." It turns out that customers visit sites like Autobytel.com at two distinct points in the decision-making process. First, they look at the site as step one in the process, to get a general idea of competitive pricing and features. This arms them with accurate information, so that when they visit showrooms to kick tires and take test drives, they already have an idea of what they will buy and how much they should pay for it. Then, when they have decided on the exact model they want, they use Autobytel.com to get the very best deal available.

By thus "crossing channels" in midstream, they usually wind up with a price that is far lower than the price they might have paid at a traditional, nonelectronic dealership, and they are assured of getting the "mass customized" vehicle that they want. So a principal lesson of this site is that cyberselling need not cancel out your retail business; following channel hybridity, it may actually complement it.

Ira Motor Group. A second, lesser known example comes from Ira Motor Group. Spurred on partly by the success of Autobytel.com and other car auctioneers, Ira Motor has constructed a profitable fusion between the fluidity of the Web and physical inventory.

While the company continues to manage the nine brick-and-mortar dealerships that have made it successful, it recently outfitted all its showrooms with Web-based technology that will let buyers preview and eliminate before ever seeing a salesman. Each dealership now boasts a bank of touch-screen computers on which customers can browse inventory data, investigate model options and prices, apply for credit, and get finance approval.

The system will even print out the preliminary paperwork for final negotiation and signature by an "analog" salesperson. But everything up to that point can be done online, which reduces the stress on the customer and the cost for the dealers: Using the Web, according to information systems vice president Bob Staretz, saves several hundred dollars in sales costs per transaction.

Notice that, as with Autobytel.com, there are still showrooms, and there are still salespeople. But here they facilitate the sales process rather than getting in its way. In an industry often maligned as a huckster's paradise, this is no mean feat. As Staretz says, "This will be a much more pleasant way to buy a car and much more cost-effective for us." One secret of that effectiveness is channel hybridity.

"Full Customer Service" at Charles Schwab

A final example of multichannel hybridity comes from a leader in electronic brokerage, Charles Schwab. An undisputed pioneer in the Internet brokerage space, they have been offering electronic trading for over a decade and now manage 1.9 million online accounts. Although the press has tended to concentrate on flashier start-ups like the major search engines and Amazon.com, Schwab actually exceeds them in online commerce. The company's chief strategy officer, Daniel Leemon, says that Schwab customers trade $2 billion of securities online every week, making Schwab arguably "the largest E-commerce company in the world. What we're doing dwarfs AOL and Amazon.com."

Schwab's embrace of the Net was a natural move, given the demographics of their customer base. Leemon explains:

It was thinking about the customer that got us there, because the Internet initially attracted a younger, more active, more independent investor. Those are the very characteristics that our customers possess, so if we hadn't found our way onto the Internet ourselves, sooner or later our customers would have led us there. I don't know that you could say that of the Merrill Lynch customer base. Our entire business today is very E-commerce—oriented, and the trend toward online activity is going to continue. We expect that before long as many as 80 percent of our customers will be investing over the Internet. It's a channel that offers simply a huge potential.

But, as Leemon is quick to point out, it's only one channel. As phenomenal as Schwab's online growth has been, the company has no intention of razing its brick-and-mortar infrastructure.

We're now doing over 50 percent of our trades over the Net. With figures like that it's tempting to think that this one channel is about to swamp everything else. But that's a mistake. You've got to see the Net as a complement, not a replacement. It's a major channel, maybe *the* major channel for many, and a very cost-effective one, but in order for us to provide full customer service, it's got to be seen in conjunction with all our other options.

Again, this has to do with what our customers demand. We've got 1.9 million online accounts out of a total of 5.5 million accounts overall. All the razzle-dazzle of the Net aside, most accounts are still opened in branches, and most of our customers still communicate with us in multiple ways. They want to keep the option of using the Internet, the telephone, or a direct encounter. Customers look at you as one company, and they expect you to execute effectively across all channels. Complete service means respecting that.

This same focus on respecting the customer is evident in the company's actual engagements online. "Our philosophy is pretty straightforward," Leemon admits.

We believe that E-business, like all business, starts with the customer. So we try to anticipate where the customer is going and plan to be there when he or she arrives. On the Internet, that's critical. Customers on the Net are very quick to realize it if you're just sending them something as a marketing exercise. You've got to stick very close to what customers are telling you—what is actually of value to them—and design your online offerings in accordance with that principle. A random banner ad is pretty useless; a targeted e-mail about what's happening to a customer's portfolio can be powerful. But you send it only if the customer has given you permission. The Net is a customer-empowered medium, and anything unsolicited is intrusive.

For Schwab, this has dictated, among other things, a rapid expansion of services beyond inexpensive trading and an increasing personalization of those expanded services. These related trends, Leemon observes, are being driven by the competitive nature of online trading:

Our competition has been steadily driving down the cost of an Internet-based trade, and transactions themselves have become extremely inexpensive. However, we believe that cheap equity trading will become a footnote in the history of the Internet.

Online investing will be much more about providing your customers with personalized views of market-based information. As that happens, we will match the perceived value of traditional full commission brokers—except that on the Net, we're able to do this much less expensively and on a twenty-four/seven basis.

If this sounds like mass customization, that's no accident. In speculating on what the future holds for E-business, Leemon cites his company's experience as a bellwether that points to a market of infinite segmentation in which customer solutions are designed on the one-to-one model. We'll talk more about that model in Chapter 8.

From Supply Chain to Supply Web?

A final word on the fluidity of the virtual market. In this book we've spoken often about the need for partnerships—and about how the Internet is accelerating that need. One interesting corollary to this fact is that the old supply "chain" metaphor may soon be in for an upgrade, to reflect the emergence of nontraditional supply "webs." So on the supply side as well, the stable lines are being redrawn.

When FedEx takes over large pieces of a corporation's traditional distribution, when manufacturers routinely jockey among several suppliers, when spare parts are widely available through virtual auction houses, when a customer can configure a home computer with parts from three different makers—when these modifications of the traditional "line of command" emerge, you know there's something big in the supply chain works. Several software companies have already envisioned the potential here, and are marketing tools to help manage the chain more flexibly. But what they're responding to is a blurring of the traditional boundaries between wholesalers, retailers, and value-added re-sellers—in other words, a different type of channel hybridity.

How that is going to shake out remains to be seen. But bet on continued, and broadening, flexibility. We second the opinion of computer executive James E. Skinner, who says, "Customers don't want to think about channels, and neither do we. . . . Our role is to follow the customers wherever they go." That means, necessarily, into a variety of venues.

Chapter 7

Online Companies Will Become Para-Enterprises

Retail on the Internet is pretty exciting—a lot more exciting at first glance than what *Interactive Week* calls "the daily humdrum task of ordering supplies and trading goods and services with business partners." But you know what? In the wide-open fields of E-business, humdrum is huge. It's in the "maintenance" operations, not the flashy big kills, that 78 percent of electronic revenue is now being generated. And that is likely to continue for some time to come. The business-to-business market, as one marketing director puts it, "doesn't have the hype or the spikes of the other Web areas. But what it does have is the strongest long-term potential. It's pretty easy to show companies the savings and productivity gains that can be achieved by implementing these systems."

By "these systems" he means Web-based "intranets" and "extranets," and those are the systems that we will be talking about in this chapter. Implementing them entails a different set of challenges than the challenges faced by a retailer or entrepreneur whose principal goal is to reach the end-use consumer.

To begin with, there's scale. Allowing your customers to order online through your Web site, as daunting as even *that* can be for Net novices, is simplicity itself compared to designing a corporate communications model that weaves your back and front offices, your suppliers, and your strategic partners together into a single, seamless, and profitable business network—the kind of fluid organization that is really a kind of extended enterprise, or "para-enterprise." Creating a para-enterprise involves a reengineering of your internal processes, an elimination of human interventions that do not add value, and an electronic coordination of "intra" and "extra" operations that eliminates impediments to the real-time exchange of information. That's more complicated than hiring a Web master and saying, "Go to it!"

There's also a difference in market focus. While the consumer's Web is full of start-ups and "go it alone" ventures, the corporate Web shows a greater degree of maturity (that's a description, not a judgment) and a greater attention to the economies of aggregation. Alert to the possibilities of community building, many corporate E-stores may be found at industrywide "cluster sites," like Digital Market for members of the electronics community and Industry.net for professionals in engineering and manufacturing. Such aggregate Web sites are creating "communities of commerce" that serve as a means of "reducing transaction costs, solidifying relationships with existing customers and attracting new ones, serving as a low-cost global marketing tool and creating new and speedier channels of distribution."

Third, and most important, there's the matter of urgency. The retail world may be divided over the potential of the Internet, but there's little such division at the enterprise level. At that level, we're way past the "wait and see" stage. It's no longer a question of whether you should be doing business online; the questions are *how* you want to do it, and *how fast* you can accomplish it. Large companies that haven't yet gotten that message, says one Internet consultant, "are waking up and realizing they're missing out, because most of their customers are online, unlike consumers."

For companies that have gotten the message, the rewards can be substantial. Consider, as an initial example, Soligen Technologies.

Paperless Precision

Many companies that design complex products deal with manufacturers who are specialists in creating piece parts. Typically, these suppliers tend to be small and staffed by highly skilled machinists who understand how designers think. They also know how to read mechanical drawings. The drawings, two-dimensional paper representations of real three-dimensional parts, are often the only descriptive medium that these companies have as an input to their manufacturing processes. Getting a design wrong is therefore serious, and it can lead to business failure both for the company that designs the product and for the specialist manufacturer.

Seeing such risks as unacceptable, a California manufacturer called Soligen Technologies has implemented a completely paperless design-and-delivery process. Initially funded by a grant from the National Institute of Standards and Technology, the process enables Soligen to do more than 60 percent of its business online. Its internal manufacturing processes, now completely automated, include the direct computer control of milling machines and lathes that can sculpt three-dimensional metal surfaces to a precision of 0.0001 inch. Business links to customers are also automated, and completely unfettered by the risks of a pen-and-ink environment.

The advantage to customers is dramatic. Instead of working from a computer-aided design (CAD) system and then producing drawings from the output, they can now send the CAD file itself electronically to Soligen, and because it travels on the Net, it gets there instantaneously. At Soligen, the CAD file is used to generate the "tool paths" that define a series of operating instructions for the milling machines. A company using this soup-to-nuts electronic service can shorten turnaround time to almost zero, getting a prototype back in the time it takes a traditional manufacturing company to produce initial drawings. This allows immediate testing and analysis of the prototype without having to wait long periods of time between manufacturing cycles.

Recently, Soligen received a request for a quote from a large European automotive company that was interested in purchasing complex automotive manifolds. Soligen returned the quote and the company placed the order entirely through the Internet. Soligen was able to create the parts and ship them to the company within two weeks, an astonishingly short time considering that preliminary intercompany communications used to take at least that long. In another case Soligen delivered twelve aluminum transmission housings to a customer in four weeks when the customer's only existing alternative was three *months*.

Soligen was able to achieve these impressive time savings because electronic processes that coordinate different companies can eliminate many of the dead spaces in manual processes, including the universal black hole of "waiting for approval" time. Traditional manufacturers may accept that as unavoidable. Netizens counter with "No way" and cut to the chase. In Soligen's case, this not only improved their customers' productivity but significantly improved the quality of their own manufactures. The same CAD database that was used to represent the part itself was also used for every downstream operation, including machining, analysis, and simulation. Paper, with its inherent fallibility, never got in the way.

Soligen, to a certain degree, is an extraordinary example. They're already there, at the profitable edge of the electronic business revolution. What about companies that are not that far along the curve? What must they do to profit from this example? And what changes will they have to adopt in the coming years to realize an equivalent measure of cost efficiency?

There are two ways to answer that. One is to chart the trajectory of the "E-volution"—to preview the dynamic advances that computerization must bring about before the effects of E-business are fully realized. This is like looking at a train from a bird's-eye view, to gauge how fast it is moving and in what direction. The other is to explain the components that must be in place before any E-business model can really take off. This is like looking at the train from inside the cab, focusing on the various components that keep it running smoothly.

Let's look first at E-business's evolutionary trajectory.

The E-volution Curve: Four Stages to Success

In a speech intended to reassure the investing public about the strength of the U.S. economy after the fateful drop of the Dow in late October 1997, Federal Reserve Chairman Alan Greenspan remarked optimistically that future growth of the economy would come through profits that were driven by increased worker efficiency and productivity. That efficiency and productivity, moreover, would be a direct result of automating internal processes—the computerization of everything from product design to employee handbooks to expense reports—to minimize costly paperwork and the "waiting for approval" syndrome. The gross domestic product itself, was the logical implication, would be fueled directly by eliminating human bottlenecks and moving data from in boxes to digital pipelines.

Much of the reengineering frenzy of the past decade reflects this belief in the automation of internal processes as a universal tonic for a sometime ailing economy. It's a good tonic, admittedly, but it's only a start—the equivalent of a couple of aspirins and "Call me in the morning." To achieve robust, sustained productivity, we've got to begin with process automation, but go way beyond it. One scenario of that "beyond" identifies four stages toward a fully digital future.

In stage one, we fully automate all internal processes by replacing paper transmissions with electronic equivalents. Typical measures of success here include a reduction in paper output, the improvement of accuracy, and increasing the number of transactions possible in a given time unit.

At stage two, we introduce changes to selected internal processes. Here, using new process-oriented measures, we work on the reduction of product development and sales cycle time, the reduction of labor costs, and the achievement of lower open accounts-receivable days.

At stage three, we achieve fundamental business process change, not just department by department but enterprisewide, by implementing automated efficiency models like efficient customer response (ECR), just-in-time (JIT) inventory, and managed care. Measures here include changes in overall productivity, cash flow, product quality, and value-chain efficiency.

At stage four, we move beyond the confines of an individual business to leverage alliances with our business partners. The implementation of this para-enterprise stage is trickier than that of previous stages, for it requires a redefinition of business itself, the creation of new, virtual corporations, and the acceptance of an integrated set of *cooperating* processes. To measure success at this stage, we will have to look at relatively novel areas, including new sales channels, new customer support channels, changes in the company's market share through these new channels, and resulting changes in profitability. Increased use of customer feedback through these new connections will be used to drive the development of new products.

You'll notice that, in discussing this fourth stage, we've shifted from the present to the future tense. That's no accident. The efficiencies created at the first three stages of E-volution are, for many companies, already in place—they're the fruit of the process reengineering of the past two decades. But only a handful of pioneers have made it to stage four, largely because of the hesitation that many companies have in "opening up the back end" to outside suppliers.

That's where the train is going, as seen from afar. Now let's take a closer look at what's happening on board, by examining two related components of E-business capability. The first, which facilitates progress through the first three stages, is an internal component.

Profit Begins at Home: Establishing an Intranet

Before you can aspire to Soligen's type of para-enterprise efficiency, you've got to get your own digital house in order. This means establishing thoroughly efficient, thoroughly automated, internal communication processes, especially in the bookkeeping areas of ordering, receivables, and payment. Ignoring this step will mean that, once you go online, any savings that you might realize from the warp-speed medium will be instantly gobbled up by in-house bottlenecks.

GartnerGroup VP Vinnie Mirchandani has a favorite story to illustrate this. In dealing with suppliers, manufacturers have traditionally required multiple cross-verifications of purchase orders, bills of lading, and receipts—at a cost that averages probably $150 per order. Net-based document checking allows you to drastically reduce this expensive redundancy, but many businesses are reluctant to take advantage of it. Distrusting their own suppliers *and* the new technology, it's like they're driving with one foot on the gas and the other on the brake. That doesn't get you anywhere, and it's bad on the engine.

The internal automation processes that are in place now, because they use Web technology and are modeled on the Internet, are commonly referred to as internal networks, or simply *in-*

tranets. Their ability to streamline workflow can be extraordinary. Consider one of the earliest and one of the best: Microsoft's implementation of MSMarket.

MSMarket streamlines purchasing. Since Microsoft sells an Internet commerce server, with integrated security and transaction support, and since it makes a point of "eating its own dog food," the company has built an internal purchasing/payment system using its own technology as a base. Unless you're in the software business, you can't do that. But even if you've got to buy rather than "grow" your dogfood (from Microsoft or somebody else), you can still learn from the example of their world-class intranet.

Microsoft has estimated that they spend approximately $1.1 billion per year on internal supplier purchasing. This mostly involves office supplies, catering, home computers and computer supplies, and books; their larger suppliers for these items include Boise Cascade, Marriott, Vanstar, and Barnes & Noble. To handle the volume, the company spent six months developing an intranet application, MSMarket, which is now available to over 7,000 Microsoft employees and supports over 800 orders per day. The system has also been extended to handle expense reports through the same workflow-enabled technology that regulates manager approvals for purchase orders.

As a result of MSMarket, the number of order entry clerks required to support Microsoft's internal supplier purchasing has been reduced from nineteen people to two. The system has also reduced the purchase cycle from eight days to three, with further reduction expected. For expense report management, the process has been reduced to three days as well, with a check being issued automatically at the end of that time. Some people would say that this feature alone would justify the investment.

One of the keys to the success of MSMarket is the almost complete integration of E-business technology. Resource planning software provides the purchasing application, acts as an electronic gateway, and automatically generates electronic documents for payment. Today, 100 percent of that yearly $1.1 billion purchasing is performed on MSMarket, and Microsoft believes that it has already paid for the application several times over.

Microsoft has not only removed the paper associated with the internal supplier purchase, it has defined and implemented corporatewide processes to replace older ways of operating. These processes now affect almost every employee at Microsoft, and they required very little adjustment by existing employees. The new procedures, being made visible by intranet Web applications, gave every employee local and remote access to this secure intranet via a standard Internet connection. So even someone who was on the road would be able to use the new system, as long as he or she could gain access to the Internet.

As for the expense-reporting feature of the new system, using e-mail for approvals has substantially decreased the time-lag here as well. Within Microsoft, when an employee submits an expense report electronically, that action triggers an automatic e-mail message to an appropriate manager (with the expense report as an attachment), and the manager's e-mail approval then moves the process to the final step, generation of the check. Again, the time-saving virtues of digitization.

Driving efficiencies at MCI-Worldcom. Similar success has been achieved at another technology leader, MCI-Worldcom.

And there, according to vice-president of information technology Mike Betzer, management has seen a major shift in people's thinking that has implications for both internal and external business processes. Mike explains:

> Intranets have already made a major difference in the way people think about this technology. At our company, the internal stuff is so electronically driven that you couldn't escape it even if you wanted to. The company handbook, all the human resources material, expense reports, order forms—it's all on the Web; we don't even have hard-copy order forms anymore. If I'm on the road and I call my administrator for a phone number, she's not going to flip a Rolodex; she'll get it, and get it to me, over the Internet. That's becoming a standard.
>
> And it's not just personnel information. People who aren't in IT themselves aren't always aware of this, but there's a tremendous amount of very technical material that you can now store and make accessible, to the appropriate users, online. We have our technical documents and architectural plans online, so that if someone building a back-end system wants to learn from the way we've built a certain front-end system, it's all available there, without the twenty-pound manuals and the endless whiteboard meetings. Now we've got a virtual whiteboard, the Web page, that development groups throughout the company can utilize.

The immediate result, Mike points out, has been "incredible efficiencies in being able to manage projects and capital better." But there's also a major plus in terms of the learning curve—a plus that creates a valuable synergistic spin.

Because of the internal uses, people get the point much more quickly. They're hooked on it in-house, they're used to going there, and they're able to extrapolate from that to the business-to-business applications. This has an interesting synergistic effect on the customer base, because a certain percentage of customers for any business are employed, themselves, by other large businesses. They're learning the patterns of Web usage in their own work spaces, and this means that when you want to sell them through the Web, they already know how it's done.

So an intranet in effect sets up its own training. It shows the productive sector how to be more efficient consumers, and becomes in that sense what Mike calls "a driver for the wired economy itself."

Floating Titanic. You don't have to be a software genius to ride the networking wave. Look at the intranet experience of a very different company, the Los Angeles film production company 20th Century Fox.

When Fox's 1997 blockbuster, *Titanic,* entered production, it quickly became apparent that the movie's unprecedented scope was creating a diseconomy of scale in asset tracking—the Hollywood studio's version of inventory control. The hundreds of period costumes, replica props, and not least of all the countless pieces of director James Cameron's 90-percent scale replica of the ocean liner were all studio property that had to be accounted for, yet they were purchased from and stored in a variety of places, making inventory look more like a rummage sale than a business operation. The film's six production supervisors (most movies have one) were reaching the end of their patience when the studio heads woke up and hired a database developer, Rod Henson, as IT director.

Henson went to work not with a pad and pencil, but with a digital camera, taking Web-compatible pictures of every lifeboat, every china setting, and every deck chair he could find. Then he entered the images into an intranet database designed by Filemaker Inc., cataloged them under 850 different entries, and presented the studio with an electronic solution that made every previous attempt look merely laughable. With his digital inventory control, any Fox employee with clearance to access the database could locate the tiniest prop at the click of a mouse, and determine whether it was going to be sold, or already had been.

The sale status of the items was not incidental. If the film had failed at the box office, Fox was planning to sell off the assets to offset its losses. For that, it needed a catalog of high-quality images, and Henson's digital inventory filled that bill. As it happened, of course, *Titanic* was no bomb, which made the hardware-software outlay for the digitized inventory a mere drop in the studio's $200,000 budget (final production and marketing costs were $300 million). Fox was so impressed with the capabilities of the system that it is adapting it for use on other productions.

It's not just Tinseltown mavens who might learn from this example. Making digitized imagery available on a company intranet can be a powerful tool for enhancing general business productivity. Ask Ron Rappaport, a Zona Research analyst who praised the Fox solution as a model that paperless-office chasers are bound to follow. Such an intranet model, he says, helps employees "conduct their business without getting caught up in the day-to-day hassle of being organized. . . . It allows them to compress information in the physical world, such as papers in a file cabinet, into a digital world so that information can be easily accessed, organized, and delivered in a fashion that does not consume the time, resources, and energy of delivering it physically."

Less paper, more time, more information. That's a pretty good description of an effective intranet, whatever your business.

From Intranet to Extranet

Once you've got your intranet up and running, you're ready for the second component of corporate E-business: linking your company's efficiencies with those of your partners. Getting there corresponds to the fourth stage of E-volution, and the way that you get there is to build what Silicon Valley calls an "extranet." An extranet is what you get when you extend Internet-supported access to your internal processes—or selected processes—to your customers, suppliers, or other privileged business partners.

For many businesses, this is a scary prospect, and in certain cases the fear may be justified. But that's a business problem, not a technological one. In fact, technology solves it, because when you move from intranet to extranet, access to your company's information—*or any part of it*—is completely controlled by you, down to the finest detail, through the infinitely malleable magic of Web site design. This aspect of Web-based business is not universally understood, so let us clarify by pointing out a critical distinction.

There are actually two different types of corporate Web sites. On a *public* site, you will see all the information that the company wishes the general public, including its prospective customers, to see. Depending on the company, that will mean a corporate overview, a product list, executive biographies, an annual report, press releases, and so on. It could be brief and flashy, or quite extensive. But because by definition a public site is open to the public, it will never include proprietary or privileged information.

A *private* site, on the other hand, is full of such information. Here the company may publish discount schedules, advance-of-release new product descriptions, or interactive demos. Private sites are full of "For Your Eyes Only" information—information that the company wishes to reveal only to trusted partners and trusted insiders. For this reason, *you cannot get to these sites* unless you fit into one or another of those categories. To access a private site, you need a special password, and you earn that password by virtue of a privileged association. The private site's owner decides who gets in the electronic door.

With that in mind, it's easy to see how an extranet can bring extra value to a business-to-business relationship. When you're dealing with a trusted partner, you don't fear efficiency; you want all of it that you can get. If you're a purchasing agent, you want access to cost and spec comparisons without having to place calls to five different suppliers. If you're a supplier, you'd like your customers to be able to order without hassles, and for their checks to be expeditiously approved and cleared. If you're a reseller, you want up-to-date discount and product information. Whoever you are, you want the right information, and you want it now. What everybody in business always needs is perfect data exchange.

With a number of notable exceptions, we're not there yet. To see why, let's look at the currently most widely used data exchange system. It's called EDI, and while it's certainly an improvement over the old paper-trail model, it's merely a stop on the road to perfect E-business.

Warming Up: The "Pre-Net" Model of EDI

The speed of the Internet causes people to speak of electronic-based business as if it were brand new, yet in one sense it has been an everyday reality for tens of thousands of companies since the late 1960s, when electronic data interchange (EDI) was first proposed. Born in the days of mainframes and intended to eliminate paper from business transactions, EDI has been used successfully by many companies that exchange big-value purchase orders, acknowledgments, delivery advice, invoices, and other routine business documents electronically and in large numbers.

The original goals were to cut administration costs dramatically and reduce human involvement in the process to zero. Manual methods of business, still seen too often today, require purchase orders to be created and printed by humans, sent by snail mail, sorted at the receiving end, and reentered into another computer system. With EDI-supported electronic commerce, orders and other documents can be sent and received within minutes. Savings from this first step alone have been significant. In the old, paper-shuffling model the typical purchase order cost $55 to process; with EDI, that number comes down to $2.50. For a company with a high volume of transactions, that might mean savings of $200,000 or more a year.

But while EDI pioneers may have invented electronic trading, EDI itself cannot be the final answer, and this has become abundantly clear since the rise of the Web. Why? Because EDI, for all its innovation, is still stuck in its mainframe-centric past, still relying too much on proprietary hardware and software. This makes it difficult, and expensive, for smaller companies to participate in EDI transactions.

EDI works by allowing different computers to exchange transactions using standard formats. These formats specify standard fields for purchase orders, shipping documents, invoices, payments, and hundreds more types of data transactions. These transactions are put typically into flat files, "batched up," and sent over a dedicated phone line or a third-party proprietary network. To be part of EDI, companies must painstakingly link their back-office systems to EDI software, then synchronize protocols with their trading partners' systems. The rigid and complex formats don't fit well with modern applications. And, although large amounts of data can be transferred, this happens at a pace that is glacial by today's emerging standards.

The cost of sending this information is also prohibitive to all but the largest companies, with a typical charge of $25 to transmit 1KB of data. It is not unusual for a company utilizing EDI to spend tens of thousands of dollars per month just sending purchase orders and invoices. The cost of necessary proprietary hardware and software required to be part of this cooperating family of businesses also adds significantly to the cost of using EDI. Compared to the Internet, which is free, this isn't a bargain.

Today, EDI is being ported to the Internet by some vendors who believe that this will give it a new life. Rather than sending forms back and forth on costly proprietary networks, companies can use products like Premenos's Templar to send EDI transactions directly through the Internet. Templar encrypts these transactions and requires knowledge of the encryption key to "unlock" the data on the receiving end. But the sending and receiving companies must still share the same proprietary software and must constantly coordinate their operations. Not exactly a boon to spontaneous commerce.

The Internet, on the other hand, offers ways to reach thousands of new suppliers and buyers and forces them to have nothing more complicated than an Internet connection and a Web browser. It can also go far beyond EDI in terms of business communications, having the capability of coordinating the entire purchasing cycle from product information on the front end to customer support on the back. In addition to this, it can carry out low-level transactions such as purchase orders through easily written, or inexpensively purchased, programs.

The Compaq Example

Here's an example, from a valued Siebel partner. John White, the former chief information officer of Houston-based Compaq, explains that his company's involvement with the world of E-business began where many companies begin: with EDI.

> Compaq's use of electronic commerce goes back about ten years, when we adopted EDI technology. Compaq was a very early user of that technology, and it has been a very long standing method for us to buy and sell product, especially in the United States.
>
> For the last five or six years, over 95 percent of all our U.S. orders—whether they're placed by a customer or a distributor or a channel reseller—have been taken electronically through elec-

tronic data interchange. We work with our suppliers through-out the world in the same way, in that we send them an electronic signal to say this is what we need to buy and they send us back acknowledgment about when they can deliver it. So we have a whole series of transactions—buy and sell orders, invoices, shipment notices, change notices, purchase orders, sales orders, all those kinds of transactions—all of them done electronically through EDI. We have supported those transactions both from the customer side and the buyer side for many years.

While almost all of our orders come in electronically, we are also enriching our use of the technology and expanding its use. From a cash application standpoint, we apply our cash electronically. Our cash payments are made to banks and we receive notification of cash payments electronically. Essentially all of our receipts are done electronically. Only a very small percentage of our order taking still uses paper.

As far as EDI goes, then, we're one of this technology's poster companies, although a lot of companies, of course, have also made extensive use of EDI. Our business model really facilitated this, because we were working with high tech companies, and a relatively few large customers represent a large portion of our business base. It was natural that we develop electronic communications between ourselves and our suppliers, because people on the high end business side are pretty well enabled with the technology and they can support it. It's more difficult to do it when you have smaller suppliers, because they don't usually have the technology or the capability of moving swiftly.

Compaq's investment in EDI, John points out, was made at a time before the Internet really took off. That has meant some rethinking of the company's electronic presence as the stakes of extended enterprising have continued to rise. What was adequate in the early days of Internet expansion—that is, five or six years ago—is fast becoming obsolete as the technology matures. As John explains, one advantage of keeping up with the maturation is that Compaq is now finding a solution for a troublesome "puddling" problem:

> Today, most of our EDI transactions are not done through the Internet. Most are done through the classical value-added network that sells services to connect buyers and sellers. We contract with this communication service provider, and we flow EDI transactions to that provider, and they manage the secure mailboxes that in turn distribute EDI transactions to the appropriate designation. The service providers are basically brokers of electronic transactions.
>
> What is happening with the Internet is that these brokers are now becoming unnecessary middlemen: Through the Internet, we can engage directly with our business partners. It's not automatic, in that the buyer and seller still have to agree to common standards and they have to agree to how they're going to exchange the information. But once you do that, you get much lower cost, and you also eliminate the "puddling" of information, which is the industry term for the delay that you get when information flows from point A to point B and then just sits there until it reaches a threshold that will kick it over into the next conduit.
>
> In many EDI transactions, the buyer and seller are on different value-added networks, and so the information goes from the first partner to the first value-added network and it puddles in that network and then it flows over to the other network, where it puddles again until the other partner receives the in-

formation. For Compaq, this is a familiar and serious problem. Let's say we have an order that we want to ship by the last day of August. After we get the electronic order from the customer, we'll translate it electronically into a production order for one of our Far East partners. They'll inform us of the production schedule, we'll send them shipping instructions, they'll send us notice that the product has been shipped, which will trigger an automatic invoice in our order management system. All of this is done electronically, so that we invoice the product and get credit for that shipment in the August reporting period.

But if the EDI transactions puddle, it throws off the reporting. Our auditors have a very strict cut off rule that says shipments stop at midnight; anything that we ship after that point we can't take credit for in that accounting period. So a puddling delay of even fifteen or twenty minutes could make a difference, especially if you get a series of them so that it adds up to a couple of hours of delay.

As we replace EDI with Internet-based exchange, we'll establish instantaneous coupling between ourselves and our partners, so that we can do basically an Internet-based two-phase commit. As we commit an action here in our system, we can send a notice to them and suspend the completion of our transaction until they respond, say, from Taiwan. We'll get near real-time synchronization. That's a main advantage of the Internet. It offers so many possibilities for being able to enhance the electronic transaction capability.

So what's the future of this pioneer solution? The answer depends on whether you're established or just starting on the Web. Although some have predicted that EDI will suffer a rapid demise once E-business starts to roll, it is highly unlikely that the huge superstructure already in place, costing many millions of dollars for installation and training, and supporting existing paperless transactions, no matter how creaky, can simply disappear overnight. The greater likelihood is that companies already invested in EDI will continue to use it until a complete, easy to use replacement is available. That may not be for some time.

For new players in E-business, however, EDI is a dinosaur. If you're just moving, or thinking of moving, online, there's little point in considering this limited and costly solution, at least as it's presently operating. The wave of the future lies in Net-carried transfers—and in fact that's even true for EDI itself, which increasingly is being merged with Internet technology. By 2003, according to one estimate, over 30 percent of EDI data will be traveling on the Net. In other words, it will be traveling over corporate "extranets."

Extranets: Four Examples

Jeff Bezos, Amazon.com's CEO, observed recently that we are in the "Kitty Hawk era" of electronic commerce. Meaning, presumably, that we've got a long way to go before Net business proves it can go the distance. But, as Bezos's own success makes clear, many online ventures are already up and soaring. Increasingly, in the corporate sector, they are doing it with extranets. Here's a sampling of how this new model—in various permutations—is making E-business fly.

A boxmaker thinks out of the box. San Francisco–based Genstar Container provides shipping containers to industrial and other equipment manufacturers. Faced with the increasing commodification of its industry, the company built an extranet that allowed online customers to view container specs, check inventory, book orders in record time, and download billing information in personalized formats. It also enabled them to exchange containers with one another rather than returning them to Genstar—a savings all around. The new system wasn't cheap. Genstar sank $1.5 million into development and created a new, fifteen-person department to complete the project. But it paid off handsomely, with turnaround times dropping from a week to fifteen minutes and most applications earning back their cost within six months. The booking application, which cost half a million dollars, ended up paying for itself in a single day.

One-stop shopping in L.A. Imagine being head of procurement for a county with nearly 10 million people, responsible for buying $650 million of goods and services a year—and doing it through a paper-based system that's completely unsystematic. That was Chrys Barnes's living nightmare until 1998, when she engaged northern California software vendor Commerce One Inc. to build a Net-driven procurement program linking Los Angeles County to its 25,000 approved suppliers. With the new system, county purchasers in any one of hundreds of offices have instant access to the same centralized database, and can have their orders approved—or routed to a manager—according to built-in rules. Early benefits include a projected savings of $38 million from an "obsoleted" central warehouse, tens of millions in savings from comparison shopping, and the virtual elimination of duplicate orders. In manager Barnes's estimation, the savings are "tremendous."

"Fast or forgotten." Adaptec Inc. makes computer-storage products that run on chips imported from Taiwan. The upside is cost savings, the potential downside wrinkles in the delivery pipeline. In an industry where, as procurement VP Dolores Marcial says, "you're either fast or forgotten," quick communication with Taiwan was a business necessity. To ensure it, Adaptec built a Net-based communications system that permits a real-time flow between headquarters and Chinese partners not just of orders but also of manufacturing instructions and engineering graphics. The extranet has cut order processing time from days to minutes and delivery time from four months to under two. Adaptec has already made back its $1 million investment, and in the process improved the productivity of a trimmed-down workforce. "We didn't want people to be paper pushers," says Marcial. "We wanted them to manage procurement and inventory." Building an extranet facilitates that transformation.

Virtual conferencing. Like Adaptec, David K. Burnap Electronic Marketing, an advertising firm whose clients include AT&T and NCR, also leverages the value of digital graphics. Until going on-line, Burnap artists would overnight color concepts in advance of teleconferences, a process that fell afoul of delivery glitches as well as the hectic schedules of frequent flying managers. With the adoption of ichat Inc.'s Rooms software, the company can now deliver graphics instantly worldwide, and clients can provide their feedback as the conference progresses: a split-screen design allows for real-time conversations (as in a WWW chat room) while Burnap and its clients are actually viewing the graphics on their browsers. Naturally, all of this extranet access is password-protected.

The system is flexible enough to allow properly authenticated third parties—project subcontractors, for example—to be cleared into the chat rooms to provide their input. To David Baker, Burnap's technical development manager, this is a major boost in Net capability. "Try to bring someone in from Wichita and not tunnel them through the Internet, and the expense is extraordinary," he says. "But when they're on the extranet—bam!—they're just tunneling through the firewall, logging in and doing their development work." Again, it's the *reach* of the Net that provides this flexibility.

Bringing It All Together: E-Business's Shining Star

Let's end with a famous example—in certain measurable ways, it's the most famous of all.

A global leader in the technology of Internet infrastructure, Cisco Systems has been called the shining star of business E-commerce. Through brilliant thinking, imaginative technological innovation, and hard work, Cisco changed itself from a brick-and-mortar seller to a virtual enterprise in about three years. In 1997, Cisco accounted for the majority of E-business conducted throughout the world all by itself, generating a whopping $3 billion in revenue. Today, its online sales are well over double that amount, and the company has become a principal actor in the online revolution. Over two-thirds of its current business comes from its Web site, and there's a target of 80 percent or more by the end of the century.

Why were they able to make this transition work so well and so quickly? Partly the reason has to do with the nature of their business; Cisco is a market leader in the construction of routers, high-tech devices that are responsible for handling the data of the Internet. But more than that, they worked consistently toward a very precise goal, making them a model for other companies who aspire to Internet success.

Cisco's success began, logically enough, with the building of an intranet—a task that involved the automation of the company's entire infrastructure. Overseeing this task was the company's chief information officer, Pete Solvik, whose "mission critical" was endorsed at the top, by CEO John Chambers. The first area Solvik and his team looked at was technical support.

When Cisco made the decision to adopt an online strategy, the company was already growing at 100 percent a year. Anticipating the extra customers that the Internet would draw in, they realized that their ability to support them had to scale appropriately, and they were concerned about their ability to continue the first-class customer support that had become accepted as the company standard. (Remember the overload problem that Volvo encountered.) Alert to the possibility that the Net would inundate them with support questions, Cisco realized that the appropriate solution was in automation.

The first part of the solution was a dial-up bulletin board system, which allowed customers to begin to support themselves. The system initially did quite well, Solvik recalls, but it began to hit the wall fairly quickly, a victim of the company's mounting success. In 1992, the team ran into Mosaic, a browser developed at the University of Illinois, and someone saw its value as a replacement for the bulletin board system. Part of its value was that Mosaic was free.

Keep in mind that, at the time, the Web didn't exist. That's how far ahead of the curve Cisco was. They started doing major development work with Mosaic in 1993, and they brought their first online site up in early 1994—nearly a year before the first commercial browser, Netscape 1.0, went to market. In a conversation about their experience, Solvik was passionate about what the Cisco team had accomplished.

> Today, we have 70 percent of our technical support and 90 percent of our software distribution taking place via the Web. We encourage our customers to use the Web, and to use it as easily as they use ATMs. We know that people prefer self-service so, just like ATMs, we're available twenty-four hours a day, seven days a week, wherever you are. Right now our technical support business is approaching $1 billion in revenue. It has a lower gross margin than our product business, but a higher net margin.

This technical support phase of Cisco's move to the Net was an unqualified success, leading to one of the best customer-support systems in the industry. The next step was to extend the automation principle to the broader area of customer service transactions, including everything from selecting a product to paying the bill. This brought Cisco into the forefront of para-enterprises. As Solvik explains, Cisco's success in this phase had a lot to do with their reliance on software applications known as "agents," which were able to perform the same tasks as human customer service agents, only faster and more efficiently:

> The first agent we put on the Net was the status agent. It allowed you to go on the Internet, enter a P.O. number to find

out what the status of your order was, and if it was shipped, hotlink directly to FedEx or UPS and get the exact location. We introduced this hotlink concept, and it was because of us that FedEx, DHL, and UPS changed their Web sites to support a direct hotlink. Now, if you're looking for a Cisco order, you don't even have to go to their sites and type in a tracking number. Our site will hotlink you right to the result.

Because the status agent was successful, we started introducing new agents every three months, approximately. The pricing agent, the lead time agent, the configuration agent, the order-placement agent, the invoice agent, the service order agent, and the service contract agent. So eventually we had about eight agents out there, collectively offering a complete E-commerce solution.

Notice two things about this description. One, it defines a commercial arena in which virtually all transactional functions, from initial query to follow-up service, are run smoothly and automatically over the Net. We'll explain the potential of agents a little more fully in a later chapter, but Solvik's catalog of wonders is a good place to start. It shows how much can be accomplished in eliminating paper drag if you combine a sound business vision with the latest Web technology.

Two, notice the importance of "linking" to appropriate partners. When Solvik shows justifiable pride in Cisco's introduction of hotlinking, he's speaking about more than a technological innovation. Linking is a software feature, but it's also a philosophy, and Cisco's investment in connections to its major carriers is part of a broader approach to business in general. Like every other business-to-business online leader, Cisco knows that cyberspace is too vast a territory to permit any company to manage it all on its own. So they've taken the notion of partnering to a new level.

The company's CEO, John Chambers, in fact, speaks of network partnering as a key to survival. "It is our view," he said in a 1997 keynote speech, "that those companies that don't understand how to partner, acquire, and do joint ventures will get left behind. And when you begin to think about the partnerships that you're going to need, they'll be the network. . . . You're going to see a generation of partnerships."

Those partnerships will have to be built on mutual benefit. In cyberspace as in physical space, customers need tangible reasons to become part of your team. In the Cisco Web experience, as Solvik reflects, the reasons had to do with those old standbys, saving time and saving money.

In the first implementation, we provided the ability to access information and asked our customers to do it all themselves, rather than make us do the work. So, the biggest beneficiary was us. They were only the secondary beneficiary.

The wins for us were immediately significant. We reduced error rates coming in, reduced paperwork, reduced time, and concluded business more quickly and more accurately. It represented a big benefit for Cisco. But our customers benefited, too. Even for the customer who just used the new system to configure a product and attach it to a traditional P.O., they had a better chance from day one of the order being correct, and not having to go back and forth to get the configuration right.

The second benefit, both for us and for them, was time. It took three days off the lead time of a U.S. order, six from an international order. So for them it shrunk time, gave them more accuracy and visibility. Still, they've got to put it in the purchasing system, and do the configuration. It's a fair amount of work for them. But obviously, all things considered, they feel that it's worth it.

With this strong sense of partnership in place, Cisco is now looking carefully at the next stage of their own growth and evolution as an E-business. And this, says Solvik, means appreciating the importance of individual customers, of providing the electronic equivalent of mass customization:

> As companies become bigger and head counts become more expensive, companies try to reduce layers of management and decrease overall headcount. They also become much less personalized in their customer relationships. As a result, the custom effort you would have done to get business twenty years ago is something that most companies won't do any more, because it's too expensive to operate that way. Instead, they say, "Here's our standard product; here's our standard purchasing contract, here's our standard price discount methodology. Don't ask for anything more." Companies are doing this because they're trying to get their organizations to operate more efficiently. It's really a "one size fits all" philosophy—everything's trying to go generic.
>
> But thanks to the Internet, there's a potential reversal of that track. Because it's electronic, you have no problem building a custom relationship.
>
> Let's say your biggest customer in the world says, "You know, I want you to put serial numbers on the box before it gets here. I want the label on the side to be custom for me, so when it comes to the receiving department, it's got the building num-

ber or the zip code or the asset number on it." And, that's a customer you need. Will you do it? Can you afford to do it? You bet. In the competitive world of the Net, you can't afford not to.

Sales are all about custom relationships, and although it's difficult to manage this manually, it's amazingly easy to do it right on the Internet. So when your customer says, "This is what I want the label to look like, and these are the fields I want," you can accommodate that. You can also establish a much more efficient communication mechanism between the two companies, one that's based on electronics rather than on paper, faxes, and phone calls. And this in turn allows you to move to the next step: that of what we call relationship management. Thanks to electronics, we're building customer relationships, entire order capabilities, that make us more customer-centric, customer-friendly, customer-focused.

We're also doing that from a product perspective. We're building in a deep connection between Cisco and each of our partner companies. We can now know the products they use, what versions of software are on them, what the status of their technical support problems are, and what the status of their network is. They can then connect with us for the next level of technical support, where we'll proactively be looking at what's happening with their use of a product, and warning them when appropriate.

Perhaps they want to upgrade a certain product. Wouldn't it be great if when they came onto our Web site, we could say, "Because we know your current configuration, we can sell you something exactly right, rather than have you buy a board and hope you've got room and the RAM's right and the power supply is big enough." And what if we had an inventory of their network, if we knew what their existing product was? We could then configuration-check the upgrade. So, it's this whole area of taking responsibility for the customer-vendor relationship, of being more direct, of being proactive, that's emerging as important.

Our long-term vision is that our customers don't have to go to us to get the order status; rather, we inform them when there's a change in the status. So, they have a dashboard to Cisco from a technical support perspective. The dashboard says, "These are all your tech support cases. These are bugs that have been found in the version of the software you're using, so you'll know about them before they start bugging you. These were your open orders that are on credit hold. This is your accounts receivable profile with Cisco, and how much open credit you have for resale. These are orders you have sent us. This is your purchase history."

With the data-management capabilities that we have available today, we can monitor and inform our customers almost instantly whenever there's a change in the relationship that they ought to know about. This is really the long-term concept that we have in mind.

Because it's happening in cyberspace, this concept may sound futuristic. It's really not. It builds on the best intentions of traditional business—a company's absolute dedication to making its customers more successful—by relying on today's technology to make it more than an intention.

That's what Cisco is really about. It's what all E-business, at its best, is really about. And it's what makes Web-based technology more than technologically impressive, that turns the Net not only into an engine of profit but also into a guarantee of satisfaction—the highest degree of customer satisfaction that the world has ever seen.

Chapter 8

The Net Will Move from Communities to "Customerization"

A community is a place where people come together, generally to serve a common purpose or share like interests. In the early days of the Web, it was hoped that cyberspace itself would become a free-form, no holds barred planetary community— Marshall McLuhan's global village, held together by computers. We now see the Internet as a host for multiple communities, each defined not by geography but by mutual interests, and we are astonished (at least we should be) by the variety of those allegiances. The infinite marketplace allows a bewildering range of user interests—too wide a range, say its conservative critics. It is fair to say that, however abstruse, quirky, or idiosyncratic your idée fixe, you can find, somewhere on the Web, people who share it. And the technology is supremely designed to help you find each other, to weave out of isolated strains a community voice.

As an E-business professional, you must begin with that fact. Then focus on finding and growing those cyberspace communities that are most obviously suited to help your business grow too.

Community Knowledge

This means leveraging what Don Peppers and Martha Rogers call "community knowledge," that is, knowledge that an enterprise acquires about customers with similar tastes and needs, "enabling the firm actually to anticipate what an individual customer needs, even before the customer knows he needs it." Their chief example is the Firefly music site, from which music lovers can elicit recommendations about CDs (and, more recently, videos) that they might like, based on the common tastes of their "affinity groups."

These groups are neither conscious nor objective phenomena. They are constructed by Agents, Inc., the Web site's owner, based on profiling information that each visitor supplies and that is entered into a database to identify (actually, to create) the groups. Because of the computational precision of database management, the profiling can be more niche oriented than conventional user surveys, and the virtual communities identified much sharper target markets.

With a conventional market survey, for example, you might check off "Country" on a listener-preference form and find yourself the recipient, within four to six weeks, of a special offer for the latest Garth Brooks CD. Sounds reasonable, doesn't it? But suppose you're one of those traditional bluegrass lovers who feel that Garth Brooks ought to be horse-whipped for killing "real country"? The CD offer wouldn't grab you, and it might turn you off. The Firefly profiling system would avoid that problem. With the speed and precision that only computers can supply, it would identify you as a member of a specialized taste group. And it wouldn't waste everybody's time by sending you broadcast messages.

The direction here, of course, is toward customization. But while that may sound like the opposite of community marketing, it's actually a more refined form of the same process. To get to any customer, one to one, you've got to begin by identifying her interest group—which implies differentiating it from ostensibly similar groups. The vast reach of the Net, coupled with the multidimensional analysis capabilities of today's customer management systems, enables you to do that with great efficiency.

In helping you to locate communities on the Web, you might want to check out a company called DoubleClick *(www. doubleclick.com)*. Serving as an intermediary between Web site owners and advertisers seeking very specific target audiences, the company has built a "network within a network" of clients like Quicken Financial Network, Excite, and United Media, who hire DoubleClick to supply a supplemental advertising stream. To advertisers, DoubleClick offers the capability of identifying markets based on a wide range of parameters, including geography, service provider, organization size, personal interest, hours of use, domain type—even the individual user's operating system.

Because of the precision implicit in this approach, results come more quickly and less expensively than in traditional ad channels like direct mail. "Because of DoubleClick's targeting capabilities," writes Chuck Martin, "companies using the service receive results almost instantly, enabling them to test market products to specific consumer groups overnight and ramp their business accordingly." That's a tremendous advantage in finding and building communities.

From Community to Communication

If the Firefly site is a model of community building, it also illustrates the value of communication. The Agents Inc. profiling system allows the company to listen to what customers are saying and then complete the loop by providing them with detailed information that will enable them to make intelligent purchasing decisions. Net-based businesses have a great opportunity to make such customer communication a living reality. E-business has got an edge on the analog world here, because of its comfort level with interactive technology.

Enterprise relationship management, our own community, has been at the forefront of developing this technology, and our success in streamlining the efforts of corporate call centers, for example, has been directly related to the sophistication of computerized profiling. Not too long ago, if a customer made multiple calls to a company's 800 line, she had to be newly identified every time. With automated customer management, that has changed.

Today, when you call a networked company for the second time, the information that you gave the first time is in the system, and the agent who takes your call already knows something about you. So his initial question doesn't have to be "What is your name?" He can move directly to a second level of communicative competence: "Good morning, Mr. Ryan. Are you calling in response to the documentation that we sent you on April third about the System 110?" With automated customer management, we learn from past calls. Every time a customer calls, we learn a little more—and we are that much abler to respond, to interact, to communicate.

With the capabilities of the Internet, it gets better. Think of profiling customers automatically, without even talking to them. Think of the refinements that you could make to your learning curve if, whenever a customer clicked on your electronic storefront, you were able to tell, in an instant, who he was and what his interests were. Think of how smart you could get about your customer base if each visitor to your site came carrying a personal history of the "taste and interest" stops on his or her cyberspace journey.

Aptex Software, based in San Diego, is a pioneer in the technology that makes this possible. The recipient of a coveted Award for Internet Marketing Excellence from the Houston-based Tenagra Corporation, Aptex has developed a software called SelectCast for Ad Servers. Sitting on high-traffic sites (Aptex clients include two of the major search engines, Infoseek and Excite), SelectCast analyzes visitors' clicks in real time and uses the resulting profiles to identify target audiences. It does this, as Tenagra notes, in a dynamic fashion:

> Profiles are updated on the fly to continuously fine-tune ad delivery. The software targets audience by developing profiles for all site visitors, and analyzing and grouping profiles to identify users with similar interests. The software then delivers designated ads consistently to users in selected groups. This "affinity modeling" process also identifies new audiences automatically as they emerge.

The success of this affinity model has already been significant. One SelectCast user, PC Financial Networks, realized as much as a 12 percent response rate to its online advertising. Another one, Microsoft's Carpoint site, doubled the rate of its previous responses.

In addition, Aptex has stepped beyond personalization into real-time information feedback. This communication enhancement is made possible by a tracking device known as a "cookie." A cookie is a tiny tag of information that Web site owners can attach automatically to your browser. The accumulation of such cookies, as you travel the Web, comprises a detailed portrait of your tastes and interests, and when you visit a new location, or the same location for a second time, the owner can read these tags like a curriculum vitae. Tracking by cookies has quickly become a firmly established system of "listening" to customers—even in cases where the customer isn't really talking. In many cases, of course, he will be talking, and this is something that you want to encourage. You can do so simply and inexpensively by including an e-mail function on your Web site map. Just be sure that you don't make Volvo's mistake. If you ask people to send you e-mail, be ready to respond.

You can also, of course, communicate proactively, like Greet Street, which delivers customized greeting cards, and the online florists 1–800–FLOWERS. Both of these companies e-mail their regular customers timely reminders when birthdays or major holidays are about to arrive, and thanks to computerized fulfillment systems, they can do this automatically. Many companies that are not in seasonal-sensitive businesses like cards and flowers also use their e-mail functions proactively, electronically "pushing" notices of new product rollouts or special promotions to Web users who have indicated an interest in receiving such material. We've been doing this kind of thing for decades analogically, every time we respond to a bingo card. Now, because of computers, we can do it more efficiently.

"Customerizing" the Experience

"The more a company can deliver customized goods on a mass basis, relative to their competition, the greater is their competitive advantage." Stan Davis wrote that in his 1987 book *Future Perfect*, and in the several years since its publication, events have proved him prophetic. In his classic study *Mass Customization*, Joe Pine II defines this emerging business practice not only as the new competitive frontier, but as a truly systemwide paradigm shift, a transformation of the basic precepts of capitalist economies. In Pine's compelling description, mass production—the paradigm of the "American System" until very recently—achieved its dominance in a period of homogeneous markets and stable demand, when manufacturers could rely on long development and product life cycles to produce heavy volumes of low-cost, standardized products. Since the 1960s, the homogeneity of stable markets has begun to break down, customers have become both more specialized in their tastes and more demanding, and as a result traditional mass production has become a liability. To survive into the next century, companies must accept extremely short product life cycles and be able to produce—on a mass basis—the individualized products that single customers demand. They must move from economies of scale to "economies of scope."

This is a whole new marketing model. Pine doesn't exaggerate when he calls it a paradigm shift—it's that universal. You see it in industries as different as high-tech and burger-flipping, as we move from a world in which Henry Ford could offer his Model T customers "any color, so long as it's black," to one in which customers everywhere are demanding it "their way." For example, Toyota now invites its customers to custom design their own cars from modular components on a mobile CAD system. A staple of the old patent medicine business, one-size-cures-all cough syrup, is now engineered for wheezes, hacks, sniffles, and other "specialized" coughs. Edward Rensi, president of McDonald's USA, says individual store managers may now offer "whatever the environment requires"—including oatmeal and cappuccino. And Marriott Corporation, in addition to niche-marketing its hotel services through subchains like Courtyard and Residence Inn, has implemented a Guest Recognition System that stores individual guests' room preferences in a centralized database.

Because computerization facilitates mass customization, the emerging paradigm is a natural fit for the Net. Given the speed of computer electronics and the ease of one-click navigability, customers with very specialized tastes are the logical audience for online businesses. Web pages can be easily designed to provide for these "markets of one" what marketing consultants Don Peppers and Martha Rogers call one of the secrets of mass customization's success: the chance for a customer to participate in the design of his or her own product. Such participation is already a fact of electronic life, and customers have already become comfortable with it because of their years of experience with ATMs. As "impersonal" as those machines may be, they do afford each user a "customerized" interaction. And the ATM gives only a hint of electronic capability.

Mass customization is already working on the Net by virtue of the medium's infinite navigability. When you browse a Web site, or surf in and out from one site to another, you're really designing a one-of-a-kind information retrieval journey—a journey whose twists and turns and even reversals you are uniquely configuring to your interests and needs. Thus the challenge of clickitis reveals the power of the mouse. In the world of E-business, customers are naturally empowered to request quite specific products and services and customized solutions, and the more your company can do to make this request process easier, the more competitively positioned you will be. The best Web sites make it easy for the customer to have it her way.

This goes not just for information, but for product specs and ordering, too. At the cutting edge of E-business, we offer customers the chance to configure their own purchases. Virtual Vineyards and Amazon.com do that in a shopper's paradigm by allowing customers to fill online "shopping carts." Following a paradigm originally established by Dell, various computer firms now offer the same high degree of customization by allowing customers to build and order their own computer systems online. There is no compelling reason that major manufacturers cannot employ the same model, for corporate as well as individual customers.

Customizing for Individuals and Enterprises

One example is Houston-based Compaq, whose former chief information officer, John White, explains that the company's mass customization efforts extend to both the "private" and the "public" Web sites that we described in the previous chapter.

> If you're an individual interested in buying a computer, you just go to our Web site, go to *www.compaq.com*, and click on

products and we'll tell you how to buy the product that you want. That's going to be the innovative use of technology, and the people that make that kind of purchase the easiest to do and the most reliable and the most inviting are going to win in the Internet commerce space. For our business partners, it's the same principle, but with a very different order of magnitude and different interface; that is, different screens from the ones an individual would see.

We have built a model for electronic commerce which provides solutions for three primary target markets. One is our reseller partners, our major channel partners; a second audience is commercial account partners; and a third is the open-market consumer. We have built electronic commerce tool kits that do various things, including product catalogs, configurations, pricing, product specification, availability, and problem resolution. Each one of those provides a bundle of capabilities, and we pull them together and present them to the partners in different ways depending on the personality and the sophistication and the price list for the particular type of customer. Naturally, we have different products and different prices when we're selling something one-off to an individual than if we're selling 1,000 pieces to a commercial account or 100,000 pieces to a reselling partner.

But the software that manages all that is actually the same software. So we've built toolkits to be able to provide very flexible support for order statusing or securing on-time delivery or just getting the product information to our customers. For each of those markets, we have built an audience-specific personality. We don't expect all our customers to have the same needs, and so we present ourselves to them appropriately; that is, differently according to their specific requirements.

When we're selling product to a commercial account, Siebel for example, we expect that everybody in that account is intended to have the same or very similar devices, because you've got the same applications and you want to have compatible equipment. Therefore, with commercial accounts, we tend to specify four or five products for each customer. When people get on the extranet, we present them with a range of options—large desktop, small desktop, laptop, and so on—along with a choice of pricing options, based on what kind of disk drive they want and other variables. But it's generally the same product that's sold multiple times within the commercial accounts.

On the consumer side, though, we don't have any idea what that consumer wants. Because he's a one-off buyer, we offer a lot more flexibility in terms of the product configuration. The online customer may start by specifying a desktop or a laptop. Then we give them basic choices, and they can drill down to the configuration that they want to specify or select the components that will go into their product. So the configuration of the software is different depending on the personality of the audience.

That difference in personality, John points out, also works on the level of the individual customer, and this too is something that the truly customer-driven company is wise to incorporate into its marketing plans. The Internet makes this logic much easier to execute than it ever was in the days of product inserts and bingo cards.

We've started to do online profiling of our customers, and this is already proving to be of great value. With an indirect business model, in many cases you don't know who the end buyer of your product is. We've always offered a card that they can mail in or they can call the telephone number and give us information about their products, but frankly, that's something that they have to do that may be of little benefit to them, and we may only find out about who bought a particular product at the time they're having a problem with it. That's not a very attractive profiling method. So we're beginning to appreciate the advantages of Internet-based profiling.

We are increasingly putting more and more information into our databases regarding our customers so that we can keep a record of installed base. Now, when customers receive a product, they can register through the Internet, which is easier and friendlier. In addition, if somebody is shopping for a Compaq product online, we give them the opportunity right there to tell us who they are. As we go to more and more online direct selling, it's going to enhance our information profiling about our customers. And I think that's going to be a general trend in business. You're going to know more and more about your customers because of this Internet-based engagement.

Another View of Profiling

Providing his own unique spin on this general trend, Novell's CEO Eric Schmidt speaks about the emergence of virtually universal connectedness in real time. Coupled with the peculiar demographics of Internet usage, he points out, this will require, paradoxically, not a "broadcast" marketing approach, but an even more intensive use of personalization. In fact that personalization, Eric says, is built in to the nature of the medium itself:

One third of Americans say that they're online, but two thirds of American *teenagers* say that they're online. You want to know where your teenagers are? They're on AOL. And what are they doing on AOL? They're sending messages to their buddies on buddy lists. Buddy lists are the fastest growing phenomenon in the United States, and this points not just to a trend, but to a universal principle. Before long, everyone is going to be online. Everyone will be accessible, in real time, to everyone else, and everyone will be able to send messages to one another. Instantly. That's not a wild prediction. It's the nature of the medium.

So what do we do with that? It's the same question that business people were asking thirty-five years ago, with the emergence of television. Here's this amazing new medium, with all kinds of possibilities for social and political indoctrination as well as marketing, and what are we going to do with it? It's a serious responsibility, figuring out how you're going to exploit a new medium, and it's all the more amazing in the current case because, with the Internet, you can reach people, for the first time, on both a highly personal and a highly interactive level.

That's new in history. It's part of the technology that's here now, and is able to offer everyone, large and small, interactivity on a megabyte or greater level. That is what provides the single most distinct shift between the existing Internet and the Internet of the immediate future. And, interestingly, it's the characteristic that most often confuses people. The Internet may look like a broadcast medium, but it's not. It's highly personal. In the commerce space, it's me interacting with a supplier, as an individual. The marketing term, one-to-one marketing, is essentially correct.

Or at least that's the anticipated outcome. We're not there yet, because we're still working out in electronic commerce what we mean by profiles and identities.

In Eric's estimation, even though the business press and the Net itself are full of documents on one-to-one marketing, we're still in the early stages of this marketing strategy, and the technology itself is far from fulfilling the celebrated Peppers and Rogers model. The problem, he says, hinges on the fuzzy notion of identity, which is the one thing you really need to market effectively—but that so far is stuck in the "context" and "category" stage. Eric explains:

> As important as it is to understand the identity of individual customers, all we really have now is contextual identities. To Amazon.com, you're a list of the books that you've purchased. On a chat room, you're a given hobby or a set of experiences. On a sports site, you're a Redskins or a 49ers fan. It never all comes together, because it's totally different markets.
>
> The only places you might potentially put it all together into a truly individual profile would be on portal sites like Yahoo! and AOL. Of course, they're doing that. Yahoo!, for example, has 18 million people registered in their personal Yahoo! profiles, sitting in databases in various places. That information could be very interesting to a marketer, but it's not open. It's proprietary. And the value of that information is very high.
>
> As for real one-to-one marketing, we're just not there yet, largely because the Internet only just happened. The way so-called one-to-one marketing currently works, it's really nothing more than narrow casting. It's putting me with the people who have my zip code and my income level. In other words, it's putting me into that category. Is this a step in the right direction? Maybe not. Because one of the things that the Internet teaches us, very quickly, is that every human being is distinctly different, and you forget that at your peril.

Think about the great discovery of modern mass marketing. We discovered that certain subgroups—whether it's teenagers, gays, or Hispanics—have a lot of disposable income. So we create subtle ad campaigns that are targeted at all these groups. Maybe social pressures make it hard for us to acknowledge that this is what we're doing, but we do it anyway, and this is a good thing, because it helps to reach constituencies that had previously been ignored.

But what about when the target group is very, very small? We accept that we market to men and women differently because they are each 50 percent of the population, but what about members of the Flat Earth Society? Or left-handed members of the Flat Earth Society who also happen to purchase Tom Clancy novels? Do they have money, too? Or are they all poor? And how would we go about reaching them, one to one, on the Internet?

Or let's imagine that we have a product, and we have no idea who wants it. How would we go about finding out? In the old paradigm, we would have focus groups. We would pay money to Madison Avenue. How would we do it in the new paradigm? Well, we'd put up a Web site. But what would we do if nobody came? We'd advertise on Yahoo. But what if our target audience doesn't go to Yahoo?

We're only at the first stages of beginning to understand this, of getting a handle on how to target customers in the new paradigm. We don't know how to answer the question because we don't know what the characteristics of the people on the Internet are. We're not talking about the "real" individual, whatever that is. We're talking about an individual we can market to. It's very difficult to define that person precisely.

As for one current popular attempt at achieving that objective, Eric is a little less sanguine than many in the industry. The use of cookies, he believes, is a short-term solution.

> Sooner or later, cookies will go away. They don't really make sense because they're stored in the wrong place. They're stored on my computer, and my computer is not me. One-to-one marketing should be to me, not to my computer. My cookies file is a form of profile, but it only "authenticates" me if I'm on that machine. Wouldn't it be better if it were stored in a directory somewhere, so I could access it from whatever machine I was on? What I would really like is to have a profile of all of the cookies that I've ever created, and all the passwords, all the authentication, all that information in one place. Because, frankly, I can't keep track of the stuff any more. And I think that, in this case, I'm pretty typical.

So the future, as Eric emphasizes, is still up for grabs. When you ask him where it's all going, he's sagacious in his silence. "I don't know," he admits. "We're all still working this out, and I don't have a lot of confidence in Internet gurus who tell you exactly, quarter by quarter, what's going to happen. In my experience, the Net is much more powerful than any individual, any government, or any company. It has its own logic, which is built on its expansiveness and its indeterminacy. That's what makes it so interesting. These are the best of times. We don't know."

A Final Word: The Schwab Experience

For a final word on profiling and customization, let's turn to Charles Schwab again—a logical choice, given this company's preeminence in rewriting the rules of the game for individual investors. Schwab CIO Daniel Leemon, in reflecting on where they have come in ten years of digital brokering, has this to say:

> What we're doing is reinventing full service brokerage. The Internet is the perfect vehicle for that transformation, because it allows you to manipulate hoards of detailed information—historical information, real-time data, investor profiles—so that you can produce, very quickly, a customized response. There's some irony here, because to the unsophisticated investor, going on to the Internet seems like walking into a warehouse in a foreign country—there's a mass of information, and you don't speak the language. But Internet capabilities themselves can correct that misperception. They enable us to assemble the information in any number of individual ways, so that everybody gets a personal guide to the warehouse, in his or her own language. We're moving beyond stock trading to advice and guidance, and that means that we're really in the information processing business.
>
> Because we can now establish customer profiles, and because we can offer proactive alerts, we are making mass customization a cost-effective reality. The Internet is the only channel on which you can do that, and that's another irony. This vast, seemingly impersonal medium actually facilitates highly personalized marketing efforts.
>
> For example, suppose a customer is heavily invested in tech-

nology stocks, one of which has been performing poorly for the past several months. The investor might or might not be on top of that information, but with Internet-based full service brokerage, the system will notice the poor performance and—if this customer has requested proactive alerts—it can send an automatic e-mail to his or her computer, recommending better performing alternate stocks. It's all about being proactive to empower the customer, and this is where Schwab is pointing the way. It's where the Internet is going.

In summarizing the Internet's value to Charles Schwab's business, Leemon notes the distinction between toy and tool. As an early adopter of the new technology, Schwab has always been alert to its commercial potential, and has never considered it merely a fad or a gimmick.

We don't look at the Internet as a toy, but as a tool that can be extremely valuable to our customers, because it enhances our ability to provide them with the services that they demand. Of course that can be fun, too—you can be serious about this stuff without becoming somber. That's an area in which the Internet has sort of changed the rules. For most people, investing is work, not fun, but the Internet has the ability to change that, to make the work enjoyable. Internet investing is fun not like a party is fun, but in the sense that the customer gains empowerment and genuine satisfaction.

Which sounds like a winning combination, on line or off. Because ultimately, whatever your strategy and whatever your business, your most valuable asset is still a satisfied customer.

Chapter 9

The Sales and Marketing Landscape Will Be Redrawn

Back in the Jurassic age (that is, five years ago), it was widely predicted that the Net would be the death both of the sales professional and of the middleman. Web-based ordering would make the salesperson irrelevant, and direct sales to customers would squeeze all intermediaries out. That hasn't happened, and it won't. Instead, like nimble organisms faced with ecological catastrophe, sales and marketing will be forced to adapt. In fact, in the most nimble companies, this is already happening. In this chapter we'll begin by examining some of the challenges that E-business is throwing at traditional sales and marketing, and then explain how those functions are adapting—indeed, must adapt—to the world of cyber rules.

Virtual Middlemen

One new model of virtuality is the digital matchmaker, the person who brings buyer and seller together without seeing either one of them. As *Interactive Week* writer Kevin Jones has described it, these "vortex" entrepreneurs are a boon to industries where "information on price, quality, or availability is difficult to find and buyers and sellers are both plentiful and fragmented." The Web removes the complication of distance, while the entrepreneur, relying on database searchability, can present stripped-down, targeted information to both potential partners.

Realbid Inc., at *www.realbid.com,* serves this honing and presentation function in the commercial real estate market. Launched in late 1997, Realbid distills the reams of description and specifications that are commonly in play in institutional property offerings, and gives online potential bidders a quick and easy version of "first cut" criteria: Where is the property? How big is it? What's the asking price? And so on. The bidders, which Realbid draws from an ever growing database, are steered to only those properties with "high match" potential, and the sellers have access, through Realbid, to a large creditworthy audience. Thus everybody saves time. "We have a purposefully limited role," says company principal Bob Potter, "but the two to five minutes [potential buyers] spend with us eliminates hours."

In Realbid's first major coup, they helped Prudential Real Estate Investors sell a multisite warehouse portfolio. Since then, numerous pension-fund managers have become clients, attracted by the company's expertise as a niche-market matchmaker. Niche expertise is critical, as one venture capitalist observes about the vortex model in general. "The home runs," says Hummer Winblad partner Bill Gurley, "will come from people who understand all aspects of a particular industry and use the Net to capitalize on that. They aggregate context, everything it takes to link a buyer and seller in that industry."

What works in commercial real estate also works in airline bookings. Priceline, which went online in April 1998, advertises itself as a "buying service," but its model is really that of a digital matchmaker, bringing together seekers of cut-rate pleasure flights and the airlines that fly a half million empty seats every day. When a customer clicks on *www.priceline.com*, she tells the company where and when she wants to go, and suggests a price that she is willing to pay. Priceline hunts for a match in its empty-seat database and brokers a match with an airline that is willing to take the bid.

Maybe the match doesn't always happen, but when it does, there's palpable value for buyer and seller alike—and, thanks to technology, it happens in Net-speed time. In the words of Priceline spokesperson, actor William Shatner, "In just one hour, you'll know if we can get you your tickets, at your price. The airlines fill their planes . . . and you get your price. It's that simple."

It's effective, too. In its first month and a half of online operation, Priceline sold an estimated 10,000 tickets, and Relevant-Knowledge Inc., which researches Web traffic, called its digital agency one of the world's ten most visited sites. In the summer of 1998, the company was gearing up to expand its suite of match-ups to new automobiles. Autobytel.com, watch out.

For a different type of virtual middleman, check out the Reliance Insurance Company's InsureDirect Web site for a rebid of your auto insurance. Click on *www.insuredirect.com* and a virtual agent will take the usual information about your insurance needs, search for available options, and within a day submit a detailed quote. Unlike the examples of Realbid and Priceline, InsureDirect is a dedicated agent—Reliance is the only seller that it represents. But the service still illustrates the value of Net-driven automation. One satisfied customer wrote:

> In a fifteen-minute trial, my family's three cars were "understood" quickly by the system, as were more distinctive qualities such as my teenager's honor student and driver's ed status, as well as the driving patterns on each automobile, individually. When, for example, the mileage on one car didn't make sense, the system was smart enough to probe further on a real-time basis, rather than triggering a string of back-and-forth follow-up e-mails. "You told us you drive 6,000 miles a year, but the statistics you gave us suggest twice that number. Please explain."

Another lesson in mass customization, E-business style. Traditional prejudices about impersonal machines notwithstanding, this virtual agent gives extraordinarily individualized service. It doesn't hurt, of course, that their prices are competitive—a common situation in a low-overhead arena.

Electronic Gavel Wielders

Another specialized form of the virtual middleman is represented by the rise of electronic auction houses. The pioneer in this arena,

Onsale, at *www.onsale.com*, was started in 1995 by Jerry Kaplan and Alan Fisher, who were looking for a novel application of stock trading software that Fisher had developed for e-broker Charles Schwab.

Like many of its imitators, the Menlo Park, California, company originally specialized in auctioning used computers and computer-related goods. After a halting start and an expansion of its scope to encompass exercise machines, electronics equipment, and even gourmet food items, Onsale now serves as an electronic auctioneer for roughly 200 regular merchandise suppliers and a bidding "membership" of over 400,000 bargain hunters. The company fields 10,000 bids every day.

In an e-auction, as in a physical auction, sellers' items are put on the block for a specified period (anywhere from twenty-four hours to fourteen days), during which time prospective buyers put in their bids, with the items going at the close to the highest bidder. But there are differences from physical auctions—small but significant ones.

- First is a principal draw of E-business in general: the enormous reach of the Net into the infinite marketplace. It's not unusual for an item to pull hundreds of offers, and even small, specialized sites get dozens of bidders per auction.
- Second, everything from bidding to billing is done automatically. Auctioning software, following each site's business rules, kicks out bids that are lower than an item's announced reserve price, and bills the high bidders's credit card once the e-gavel falls.
- Third, precisely because of automation, overhead savings are passed to customers in the form of low commissions. Onsale's

major competitor, the San Jose–based Ebay *(www.ebay.com),* charges only a twenty-five-cent listing fee and a 5 percent commission.

Like Onsale, Ebay has learned the lesson of diversification, and it manages the sale of everything from computers to Beanie Babies. Many auction sites, though, take the opposite tack, serving as specialized trading venues for hobbyists or collectors. The Boyds and Bears Auction Board, for example, specializes in novelty gifts, especially teddy bears. Guitar Auction handles guitars; Mother Lode Gold deals in gold and gold jewelry; and Phoebus Auctions leans toward estate sales and antiques.

The Web is also host to many marketplace "newsgroups"— communities of collectors whose informal auctions serve as electronic green sheets within a surging gray market. The exchanges here happen in a direct sales model, through e-mail postings and without an Onsale-style intermediary. It's not exactly high finance, but there's a lot of it out there. And the ubiquity of this model should give business pause. It's one of the greatest ironies of the Internet age that this futuristic technology, the brainchild of big business, is facilitating the resurgence of a quasibarter system that, in the nimbleness with which it circumvents mainstream sales channels, is posing a quiet challenge to capitalist tradition. It's a challenge that alert professionals are already rising to, as they perceive in the e-auction surge an opportunity they can leverage.

Listen to Stuart Feldman, director of IBM's Institute for Advanced Commerce. Most modern businesses, he says, have traditionally locked themselves in to a fixed-price model, because distance from customers makes one-to-one bargaining a logistical nightmare, and they have been unwilling to entrust bargaining latitude to people in the field. The Internet changes that. It "allows communication at no cost and infinite speed. And you can program computers with rules for what deals they can and can't make, instead of trusting a five-dollars-an-hour clerk." The likely outcome? A price flexibility that seems more suited to an open-air market than to the intensely structured arrangements of modern-day capitalism.

But that's an irony to which businesses must begin to pay heed because, in a world of price elasticity, only the elastic will survive. Fixed pricing, as Feldman says, "is not ingrained in human nature." The online auction houses have already seen that, and they may be the harbingers of a pricing revolution. Onsale's CEO Jerry Kaplan certainly thinks so. His prediction: "We are moving to an age where business will quote a different price to every customer for every product every day."

Extreme? Possibly. But in the age of mass customization, maybe not. One-to-one marketing, after all, implies individual pricing: The "right" price is part of the package that a satisfied customer gets. Price elasticity, moreover, is a capitalist given. We see it on a year-to-year and week-to-week basis, when the price of a motherboard plummets because of backed-up inventory or the avocados go up after a late spring freeze. Neither customer haggling nor price adjustments were invented by the Web. The Web, with its infinite outreach, is just making them the norm. The auction houses are building a business on the recognition of that truth.

Selling Reborn: From SFA to ERM

Partly in response to pressure from the new virtual middlemen, but chiefly as a means of holding down rising engagement costs, sales in the last ten years have become widely automated, and sales force automation, or SFA, have become one of the most lucrative segments of the software industry. Beginning with the simplest types of automated assistance, personal contact managers like ACT and Goldmine, we have moved rapidly into the realm of virtual selling, where the information capabilities of an entire organization, from customer databases to product configuration, are available to the field salesforce in real time, through the everyday wizardry of laptops and Internet connections.

In the same brief period that it took the Internet to move from infotainment to E-business, technology-enabled selling has also taken a huge stride, from simple automation to emergent optimization. Indeed, we speak now of our industry's cutting edge as SFO—salesforce optimization. This is destined to have a profound impact on corporations.

At the very basic level of SFA, the immediate objective is the attainment of cost efficiencies. Even a very simple technology like contact management can help to reduce costs and streamline the work flow by the replacement of paper with automatic record keeping. That's what the first generation of SFA has done. It has saved businesses around the world time and money by making routine tasks truly routine; that is, by making such procedures as lead tracking, appointment confirmation, and fulfillment part of an electronically driven customer-response system that is both more reliable and more efficient than mere human memory. The goal of the second generation, the SFO generation, is to move from this sales efficiency to sales effectiveness.

Industry consultant Jim Dickie, managing partner for Insight Technology Group, describes this development in our company magazine, as he analyzes the technology choices that reflect the shift.

> If a company succeeds only in making its people more efficient, it just means that the average sales rep can make more average calls. Companies now want their average sales reps to make great calls, and their technology choices mirror that shift. The top application choices five years ago were contact management, e-mail, word processing, and lead tracking tools. Today, companies are investing in opportunity managers, configurators, marketing encyclopedias, data mining systems. These next-generation tools don't just automate what people do, to help them do more, but they also empower people, to help them do more, better.

This shift, as Jim recognizes, inevitably implies that what we mean by "sales" is undergoing a radical redefinition. The technologically fearful have warned that SFA will be the death, the gradual outphasing, of the corporate salesforce. In fact what sales technology is already bringing about is a widespread revitalization of traditional selling, an electronically driven fusion of boundaries that is linking sales and marketing with traditionally "nonselling" functions, so that the corporation as a whole can have a single selling vision. Here's Jim again:

> To successfully serve customers today, sales organizations are finding they have to minimally coordinate the efforts of mar-

keting, call centers, field sales, channel sales, and customer support. In addition, they are realizing that they need to link front-office systems with back-office systems such as finance, distribution, and manufacturing to meet customer expectations. Focusing sales reengineering efforts on the sales force has shifted to focusing on the efforts of the enterprise.

The natural trajectory, therefore, is away from sales (or sales and marketing) as freestanding, independent "functions." It's toward an understanding of sales as an integrated—and integrating—function, such that the overall goal of technology, from simple to complex, is the synergistic support of enterprise effectiveness. In this generation of Net activity, we pass through SFO to the final stage, ERM, or enterprise relationship management. The tools for making this step are all well in place, and the future will belong to those enterprises—or para-enterprises—that are the first to recognize this fact and act on it.

At our company, Siebel Systems, we acted on the fact by merging, in the spring of 1998, with Scopus Technology, the best-of-class supplier of customer service and call center applications. Under our new para-enterprise umbrella, we are now able to offer our customers total end-to-end solutions that integrate customer service, marketing, and multichannel sales management. As we put it in *Siebel* magazine, the merger was both a "win-win for current customers and an unprecedented opportunity for potential customers to finally have access to the most robust single-source enterprise relationship management systems available."

Robust, single-source ERM—that's the reality of the future in electronic business, and if you're even minimally involved in Internet commerce, it's a reality that you're going to encounter regardless of your size. The Siebel case may not be the most obvious proof of that because, even before the Scopus merger, we were a large, global company with hundreds of salespeople. But if you suspect that Net-based ERM is only for the giants, listen to the start-up experience of Salman Malik.

Beyond "Sneakernet" at Firefly

Salman, who is now product manager for Siebel Systems' Internet applications, was one of the founders of the Firefly network, the developer of community-building technology that was described in Chapter 8. Reflecting on his experiences in that small but rapidly growing business, he recalls how quickly SFA must give way to ERM.

> At Firefly, my experience was that by the time we had only five or six salespeople—out of a total of about thirty-five employees—we saw a definite need for software to coordinate their activities. At that early stage, we had five or six people who were by job title salespeople, and another five or six senior people who were involved in relationships with customers and strategic partners. Every one of these relationships was multifaceted—you had a possible technology relationship, a possible comarketing relationship, and a possible sale of advertising space on Firefly's online service or of its software technology.
>
> So you had different people talking to different parts of larger enterprises, and sometimes one person would go in and discover on the call that someone else from Firefly had already talked to the same people weeks before. Despite being a close-

knit team, we couldn't be fully informed about our multiple contacts with a given enterprise. We definitely needed an ERM technology to help us coordinate this. Much of the reason I ultimately joined Siebel Systems was because of my firsthand experience at Firefly of an almost universal business problem—coordinating enterprise relationships.

And the advantages of ERM at such a start-up enterprise? Essentially, they're the same as you would find in any global operation: greater speed, less redundancy, and more efficiency. It's something that Salman, as an avid Net watcher, sees on a daily basis, although, as he pointedly observes, at many "wired" businesses the obvious advantages of automating the sales and marketing functions may be terribly hampered by a behind-the-scenes reliance on more traditional methods.

We've come a long way in the past few years, but what's really amazing to me is the level of inefficiency that's still in place at so many online businesses. There are plenty of examples of seemingly sophisticated Web sites where you can go and purchase products just by typing in your credit card number and hitting a button. The site will then tell you, "Thank you. Your order will be shipped to you shortly." You're probably unaware that behind the scenes, what happens next is as unsophisticated as you can get.

What happens, in many companies, is that an employee gets an e-mail with all of your information in it. This person then has to print out the e-mail, go to a mainframe terminal, and re-type what you've already done for the order department. We call that "sneakernet," and there's plenty of it going on. The front end can look cool and efficient and Web-like to the customer, but behind the scenes, you actually have this archaic process still in place. And naturally the costs of serving these orders are still relatively high.

Worse than that, not only are the costs high, but there's a customer-service issue. If you've got a system designed like that, you probably cannot tell me the status of my order without my having to talk to a human being. So an architecture like that means that you can do some very basic stuff, but you're not really providing a full capability. That's what's happening at the late-adopting end of ERM management.

At the early-adopter end, of course, things are considerably better—and getting even better all the time. In pioneering companies, enterprise relationship management is providing unparalleled efficiencies to corporate work forces, dramatically increasing the effectiveness of meeting customers' needs.

It accomplishes this not just by the magic of technology—that is, the speed of Net-driven information exchange—but, much more importantly, by involving the customers themselves in the configuration process. This point was made in *Virtual Selling*, but it bears repeating, because it's really the heart of what we mean by the changed sales landscape.

When both you and the customer have "full capability," real-time access to all the information that's required to provide a mass customized solution, then in effect *the presentation is the configuration*. This is true whether the customer is buying directly from your Web site or speaking with a sales rep who is communicating with your back office through a laptop. In either case, the interactivity that Web-based selling can provide allows for an unprecedented degree of product or service customization. This both speeds up the selling and facilitates future interactions:

By the time you've interactively customized your pitch to the prospective customer's needs, you've also managed not only to gather reams of knowledge about the customer that will be useful in the future, but also designed the product that the customer wants. More precisely, both of you have done the designing—thus, your customer, by joining in the presentation, finds himself or herself two-thirds of the way through the entire sales process.

As this description should make clear, this doesn't mean that the salesperson is suddenly irrelevant. That's a common misconception about networking in general, and about sales-enabling technology in particular. When we say that the trajectory from SFA to SFO to ERM will change the landscape of sales and marketing, we don't mean that it will sweep the selling arena clean of people. On the contrary. What sales-enabling technology will do for the salesperson is what technology in general always does for skilled workforces: It will free the salesperson up to concentrate on those activities that a machine, no matter how sophisticated, cannot perform. All the looser, associational, free-form interactions at which salespeople have always excelled will still be performed by individual humans.

So the answer to the question of whether the Web will eliminate the salesforce is: No, but it will demand that you rethink carefully what you want your salesforce to do. If you find your salespeople walking around with notepads, taking orders, you'll need to ask yourself how expensive it is to have them doing that as opposed to showing your customers how to do it for themselves, automatically—and letting the humans do the work that humans do best.

The Next Stage: Agents

The flip side of this injunction is to allow machines to do what *they* do best—which, in the world of cyber rules, means the rapid recovery and manipulation of detailed information. One new and exciting way in which this is happening can be seen in the development of software agents.

We don't mean people who sell software. We mean software applications that function like human agents to filter through the "gargantuan piles of infotrash" that now clutter the Web and zero in—more quickly and more efficiently than any human agent could—on the useful data that you and your customers need. Primitive agent technology is already widely visible, in the form of today's online search engines. But in the next five years, we will go way beyond the primitive, as we see the fine-tuning of buying agents, selling agents, and their interaction.

In order to serve us well, virtual agents will have to know what we like and what we don't; they must recognize the names of those people we want to get messages from and those we would like to ignore. They will be able to find information for us automatically, filtering it specifically for our needs, finding new sources of good information. They will be capable of operating on the Internet as our virtual representatives, looking for good deals, updating our profiles, and buying specific products according to our instructions.

The technology for all of this is in place today, but it has been somewhat impeded by security concerns. As security measures become more sophisticated in the next generation, that will change. Soon we will be able to provide customers with buyer's agents that are the personal property of each buyer. This new agent technology will be totally secure; that is, all the knowledge that it gains through profiling or interacting with the buyer will be available only through the buyer himself or herself. The agent, as a software entity, and the data it uses, will be encrypted on the buyer's client machine, incapable of being copied or deleted by anyone other than the owner.

When seller and buyer agents talk, it will be the seller agent's job to get information intended to narrow the search range, such as what your preferences are, and how you will use the product. It will be the buyer's agent's responsibility to divulge just enough information to be useful, and not so much that it might impact an owner's privacy. In the early days of agent development, these questions will necessarily be put to the buyer himself or herself, because the buyer's agent won't have the depth of knowledge or the sophistication required to answer these questions. So the agent's role will be to collect general information and organize it for the buyer. Because of this, we expect the human buyer to remain personally involved in online buying and selling until agents can begin to answer these questions from the knowledge base they have on their owners, and on their ability to communicate their knowledge to other agents.

When this happens, we will not only have agents dealing with agents, but agents working on our behalf empowered to buy and sell for us, without our direct on-the-spot approval. This will be an exciting time, and will cause acceleration in the rate of evolution of E-business. It will be the dawn of a new generation of "intelligent" buying.

We're not quite there yet, but we're moving quickly, and intelligently, in the right direction. To appreciate just how intelligently, listen to an insider's view of how ERM technology has already transformed his company's customer relationships. Mike

Betzer is vice-president for information technology at MCI-Worldcom, and although he spent most of his career at MCI in sales management, he has spent the past several years—roughly the first generation of the Internet—overseeing the transition from legacy systems to next-generation technology.

The View from MCI-Worldcom

In reflecting on this shift—and particularly on the adoption of sales-enabling technology—Mike admits that, like many other IT executives, he originally wondered whether the potential would justify the investment.

> For a while, like everybody else who adopts a new technology, we were starting and stopping, feeling our way, and wondering if this was just a very expensive mail machine. You take ten thousand dollars or so for each PC or laptop, and you're talking about forty or fifty million dollars. You've got to ask, is it really worth that much money? Even today, there's still a small percentage of people who are saying, "Is this whole front-end stuff worthwhile? Why not just have people access the legacy system?"
>
> But the technology itself changes that perception. Three years ago, maybe 60 or 70 percent of our users thought that way; now, as the benefits become obvious, it's maybe 10 percent or less who are still stuck in legacyland. Overall, it's pretty widely acknowledged that the client-server model and Internet capability have dramatically improved our ability to serve our customers.

Actually, as Mike points out, this means that customers are better able to serve *themselves*. The technology enables the com-

pany by enabling its customers—by making them active participants in the sales and marketing process.

> With Web-based interfaces, you can start with a novel premise:
> Any single thing that the customer can do on his own, let him do
> it. This goes both for our consumer and our business customers.
> Whatever the size of your account, you can sign up for MCI on
> line, pay your bill, select products, manage your account—any-
> thing that you can do over the phone with a customer service
> representative, you can now also do from your PC. And it's
> cheaper. Cheaper for us, and therefore cheaper for the customer.
>
> This is not without its concerns, admittedly. There's the old
> saying that if your customers aren't calling you, who are they
> calling? So there's some uncertainty within the company about
> the Web models, and part of that, of course, is simply numbers.
> Our customers are beginning to communicate with us online,
> but so far they're not doing that in droves, which means that at
> this point it's still an emerging service model. We're pushing it
> heavily in our advertising, though, and we're confident that
> more and more of our business will be moving to the Web.
>
> It's like online banking. To some people that seemed scary at
> first, but the trend is inevitable: It's easier and it's cheaper, so
> it's also logical. For customers who use our Internet products,
> moreover—whether that means hosting or serving as an ISP or
> complete network management—the reluctance is negligible.
> They're already sold on the Net, so using it to manage their ac-
> counts is only common sense.
>
> This is especially true among our largest customers. We've
> just launched a product called Interact, which enables our cor-
> porate clients to manage and review their bills online in great
> detail, without the reams of paper that most corporate billing

entails. At the high end it's all about billing and cost containment, and large companies are now well aware that their information infrastructures aren't a cost but an opportunity to reduce costs by more efficient management. Interact and similar technologies enable a business to review its usage patterns quickly and accurately, so they can forecast bandwidth needs and resolve them promptly, before a high-usage segment turns into a problem.

This, again, is an example of empowering the customer. We can tell them, "It looks like you've got a traffic increase here, and we'd recommend that you consider more bandwidth," but when they discover that themselves, with a product like Interact, they have instant ownership. So they see their trends earlier, they forecast better, they order faster, and they control their growth better because the Internet has allowed them to anticipate where they'll be going.

It gets better. With their largest customers, Mike explains, technology enables MCI-Worldcom to set up a kind of private network *within* the Internet, which leads to even greater cost efficiencies. This has been made possible with an Internet application called an account communicator.

Take Chrysler, for example—one of our major corporate customers. Since we do so much business together, we've established a common Web page on which their telecom people and our people can communicate. We call it an account communicator. We built it together, and it includes everything each corporate team needs to know to work together—pictures, addresses, databases, phone and pager numbers, where and how to find any information anybody needs. It looks like any other

Web page, but it's dedicated exclusively to this one relationship, with access to it limited to those involved.

It's been enormously successful in a very short time, and we're now in the process of marketing it as an Internet product, as part of a newly developed suite of "On Net" offerings. The design is to let corporations go from local to national to global and back to local seamlessly along a single network—no handoffs. The market for this begins with Chrysler itself. They see how much easier an account communicator has made our relationship and they say, All right, how about our other relationships? Why not an account communicator between Chrysler and U.S. Steel, or Chrysler and Johnson Controls, which makes their seats? That's the logical extension. That's why we're working now with Chrysler and Johnson Controls (they're another of our customers) to triangulate the development of another Web page.

That's one of the exciting aspects of network technology. You get one great idea and, practically before it's rolled out, it triggers another idea. Somebody's thinking, "Wouldn't it be great if . . . ?" and before you know it that "if" has become a new product. It's a technology that enables itself, that develops itself.

Not the least advantage of MCI-Worldcom's account communicator is that it fosters the kind of sustained relationships that every business wants. The interlocking of MCI-Worldcom, Chrysler, and Johnson Controls, in fact, is a perfect example of a para-enterprise. Mike suggests that such arrangements provide a level of security that isn't available in more traditional models and that, looked at from one perspective, they may minimize competition.

We are locking our large customers in more and more, every time we establish a joint project of this magnitude. Given the capability that we can offer them online, we become—or we strive to become—the backup standard. If we do it right, nobody's going to come in and take that business away, and in a sense, therefore, such arrangements are reducing competition. Your aim is to do it so well that no competitor can shake the arrangement. That's good for us global leaders, bad for the little guys.

But, Mike is quick to add, that's just one extreme. Looked at another way, the very technology that gives MCI-Worldcom an edge in customer management also holds out an unprecedented opportunity to nimble new players.

Another possible scenario is *increased* competition, made possible by the advent of relatively cheap start-up costs. You've got small telephone companies with no Internet backbone and very little infrastructure, and if they can put up a great Web page and manage it intelligently, they can be players in this space too. The Amazon.com phenomenon isn't confined to books. In the end, what's happened reveals the oldest of all business lessons. The company that is closest to the customer, and that provides a uniquely satisfying solution to each customer, is going to win. It's not necessarily going to be the old hands, because old hands have a way of sitting on their hands, of getting superconfident and then getting outmaneuvered. It happened to Barnes & Noble, and it happened to AT&T twenty years ago, when we arrived.

Internet technology doesn't presuppose any particular outcome. In some cases, the big corporations will get it and they'll win, because like us they'll put an appropriate percentage of their capital dollars into keeping up with this curve. In other cases, the giants will fall and upstarts like Amazon.com will rewrite the rules and come out ahead. It's a very fluid, incredibly fast-moving space.

What about the *people* in this world of smart machines? What, specifically, about the salespeople who, for generations, have kept the gears of global business buzzing? Is there still a place for them in Web-based business, or—as customers are empowered to do more and more for themselves—will salespeople become as obsolete as the electric typewriter? While attentive to the problems that technology poses for traditional selling, Mike is relatively sanguine about the survival of the profession.

As things move more and more into a commodity space, the traditional world of selling is bound to change. Dell is a perfect example of that. They've said, in effect, "A PC is a PC is a PC. You can figure out what you want and here it is." But this doesn't mean that sales in general is doomed to extinction. At a certain level of sophistication—way beyond commodity selling—you may need the salesperson even more than you did before.

If you look at the high end of our salesforce, for example, you've got people who are managing accounts that are giving us one hundred thousand to three hundred thousand dollars a month. Customers like that will always want somebody close to make sure that everything's being done right. We use the phrase "one throat to choke." A negative expression, but it has a positive side. It's the one—at least one—human being to whom the customer can relate on a personal level, and to whom, very often, he or she insists on relating. To fill that role, you need sales professionals who are technologically savvy but also incredibly efficient and effective, who are unparalleled in customer relationship and management skills. At the low end, it might all be automated in another decade. But when you've got major investments involved, you need a personal touch that may never be duplicated by a machine.

The same principle applies, Mike points out, in the marketing arena. Here businesses have got a gold mine of customer-related data, but in many cases they fail to appreciate its potential because they're managing this space-age information with an order-taker's mindset. They're not fully utilizing the *personalization* that such data can provide.

We've got terabytes of data on every consumer in the country. I don't mean just MCI-Worldcom, but most large businesses. We know virtually everything about everybody because we buy it. Every customer's interests are in a database somewhere, and it's not a major chore to make that data your own. On top of that, at MCI-Worldcom, we have the capacity to call every household in the country every three months, and that gives us better data, more specific data, constantly updated. The consumer paranoia level about this can get pretty high, but the time for keeping the data private is long past. Whether you like it or not, the reality is that the data is out there. The question is, what are you as a business going to do with it?

The great opportunity here is to personalize each contact, so that when my marketing people call you, they're talking to you, personally, not just number 324 on a call list. If I know that you fly Delta a lot, and we're a Delta partner, then I may get your attention with a Delta promotion. For another customer, it's something else. But if one-to-one marketing is going to be anything but a slogan, it's got to be built on at least trying to personalize the relationship.

For example, I called one of my credit card companies recently to discuss a bill. I travel every week, and I pay this company thousands of dollars a month. Yet they see me, as far as I could tell from the phone conversation, as no different from somebody who routinely misses his due dates. With all the data they have on me, that's the best they can do? That's the problem with data, ultimately. You can have all the data you want, but if you don't give it to your call center people, if you don't give it context—in other words, if you don't translate the terabytes into *intelligence*—it's just taking up memory in somebody's hard drive. And instead of using the technology to build your relationships, you're reduced to going for the order, and depersonalizing the call.

No matter how thick your customer files are, that's a sure way, eventually, to lose business. Because those who treat everybody the same—their days are numbered. Sooner or later, whatever the technology, service prevails.

The Ultimate Lesson

Service prevails. That's an excellent statement of E-business's real eye-opener. It's that, whatever the role of software agents, and indeed of technology in general, in the networked future as in the pen-and-ink past, *only customer-oriented organizations will survive.* Commonsensical as this may sound, it may be the only "absolute" lesson of E-business's first five years. On the Web, as in any other venue, you've got to follow your customers, and only the vendors who accept that fact have a chance of succeeding.

On the Internet, it's actually easier to follow this injunction than it is to do so in the brick-and-mortar environment. Why? Because Net technology, more than any previous technology in history, can give you marketing data that is precise, up-to-date, and infinitely customized. The companies that use that data most effectively will be the ones who thrive in this highly competitive atmosphere.

More specifically, market share will go to those companies that differentiate themselves from the competition in terms of customer knowledge, customer service, respect for customer privacy, and the establishment of customer trust. Knowledge and service perhaps go without saying. Privacy and trust are somewhat fuzzier concepts, but attending to them will be essential in the next generation. If the first five years have taught customers the possibility of Net trustworthiness, the next five will allow them to identify whom they can trust. The survivors will be those companies who ensure confidentiality, and whose business practices consistently live up to the promise. If you're not ready for that commitment, you're not ready for the Web.

This last point isn't really a prediction. It's the central lesson of this book, as well as the basic key to running a business. Focus on the customer, and everything will take care of itself.

Part III

Getting There from Here

Chapter 10

Rolling It Out I

Digital Strategy

Given the scenarios we've presented in the previous chapters, you should now be convinced that the real questions to be asked about doing business through the Internet are no longer "if" and "why" but "when" and "how." The answer to the "when" is pretty easy: Do it now. Start getting a digital strategy in place without further ado, or be left behind by competitors who are already doing so.

The "how" is a little more complicated. In this and the following chapter, we'll address that question, laying out the practical guidelines that you must follow to make your E-business mission a functioning reality. We begin in this chapter with the broadest of these guidelines: the decisions and choices you have to make at the organizational level. These may be broken

out into five basic steps. To be successful in E-business, you
must:

- Define the vision
- Coordinate your internal resources
- Establish partnerships
- Coordinate your data
- Measure the effectiveness

Much of this is business-principles-as-usual, translated to the
Web, and some of it is as new as the Web itself. Let's look in turn
at each of these critical five steps.

Step One: Define the Vision

This essential first step goes back to the point we made in Chapter 3 about the need to think through why you want to go online.
Yes, the World Wide Web is an exciting place, and yes, the opportunities for business are unique in history. But it doesn't follow
that those opportunities are the same for every business, or that,
simply because the Web is there, you should jump to be a player.

Business managers whose companies do poorly in cyberspace
often falter because they've ignored this initial question. Or, even
more commonly, they think about the question and come up with
this pat answer: "Well, everybody is telling me I should be on the
Internet." Not a good reason. When Net watchers urge you to go
online, that's an excellent reason to start investigating the possibilities. But it's not in itself a good reason to follow the advice.
Instead, what you should be doing is reviewing the multiple op-

portunities that the Internet provides you, and determining which one or ones best fit with your business.

What are those opportunities? Well, the most obvious one—and the one most managers think of first—is to sell products or services directly to customers. Using the Internet as a new channel, as a round-the-clock, ubiquitously accessible cash register, is widely perceived as the lowest common denominator in the realm of E-business. If that's your intention, and if your product line lends itself to such direct selling, great. But in defining a vision, don't stop there. Remember that there's a great deal you can do using the Internet that can strategically complement your business and your competitive position but that has nothing to do with the actual transfer of goods or services. And managers frequently overlook this when planning an Internet strategy.

Often, when people think about the Internet, they think in terms first of visibility: "Brochureware is going to be our first step. Get our company brochure up there with contact information on how you can find us and where our global headquarters are." Then they move immediately to Internet commerce: "The next step must be to allow people to buy stuff from us over the Internet." That's not necessarily true. Even where it is true, it's not necessarily going to work best in a direct-sales model. Just because the Internet exists does not mean that every single manufacturer of gaskets and rubber tubing should be selling his stuff directly on his own Web page.

Because the individual Web page route is not the most appropriate route for every business, defining a vision means you should broaden your perspective. You might do this by reviewing the lessons of the first five years, as we described them in Chapter 3, and making yourself familiar with the plethora of options that beckon to anyone considering doing business online. With that information, you may decide that you do, indeed, want to sell products. You want to create a catalog of your products on the Internet. But maybe not. You may decide that a hub site is a wiser alternative. Or you may realize, like Ragú, that it's not product selling at all—that the plus for your company in going digital is not the immediate revenues, but the opportunity to educate customers, direct them to your off-line outlets, or build your brand. We've described these strategic options in previous chapters. They're worth discussing with your team before simply throwing up a Web page.

You'll also want to discuss the comparative potential of using your site to attract new customers visually and of using Internet technology in nonvisual ways, such as the completion of transactions from computer to computer that we described in the chapter on "para-enterprises." Usually, when we talk about Web sites, we're talking about only one application of the Internet, its ability to display graphical, human-oriented user interfaces—the snazzy Web pages that you see everywhere in cyberspace. But other uses of the Internet are machine-oriented rather than human-oriented—they exchange data between computers—and these are the ones that will grow rapidly in the very near future.

For example, when an intranet site displays a list of pencils and pens and other supplies, often it is actually "talking" to computers at a number of different suppliers, and then relaying this information to the intranet. That's an example of Internet activity that has nothing to do with the Web. For your particular business, is that an option to consider?

If you're targeting the acquisition of new customers, you'll have to think about how you get people to your Web site, and once they get there, what keeps them there, what makes them return, and what makes them become repeat customers. The Internet, like other channels, is about repeat purchases, so you want to make it easy for your customers to reorder. This may also mean proactively reminding them when they really ought to be reordering, even if they don't yet realize it.

There is a different set of things you might think about when you consider your existing customers or partners. For new customers, it may be important to have a lot of marketing collateral—press releases and testimonials, for example—that convinces them of the need to buy your product. For existing customers, you might want to take every dollar you'd spend on marketing collateral and instead spend it on heightening your functionality, streamlining the work flow for actually doing a transaction as well as for functions like reporting and inventory management. Rather than spending your money on visuals that describe the value of your product, when you're communicating with customers who already understand that value, you might want to spend that incremental dollar on informing them or helping them manage their inventory better, and therefore encouraging them to reorder on a regular basis.

If you're a large concern, moreover, you'll probably want both of these strategies working in tandem. You're going to want some private access screens reserved for customers and partners who don't need the graphics because they already know the rules for doing business with you, and other, public screens for your over-the-transom customers. Considerations like these help you determine what kind of Web pages you want to have—not only which bells and whistles you may desire, but also who gets to see what pages, and for what purpose.

Step Two: Coordinate Your Internal Resources

You wouldn't consider building your own skyscraper by having your finance and accounting department work overtime on moving and bricks and mortar and welding girders; instead, you'd hire an architect and a general contractor whose professional expertise would make it happen for you. In fact, you might go directly to a real estate developer and have that company develop it entirely for you, and just at the end of the day put your name on the tower. The same is true of developing your presence on the Internet. It's a complex space, so you need the help of professional service firms and professional software companies that can help you enable the particular kind of presence that you want.

But even before you do that, you've got to "prepare the ground," as it were. You've got to coordinate the people *inside* your business who will serve as the dynamic liaisons between you and those outside experts. That's step two. Before you talk to the first Web developer or Internet service provider or hosting company, you've got to create your own internal task force— the people whose sole responsibility is to manage your online presence.

This task force must include professionals who (1) are familiar with all the different uses of the Internet; (2) are creative and willing to explore the different business models that the Internet puts forward; and (3) at the same time have wide credibility within your company, because they've succeeded somehow in your existing line of business. Business professionals who can bring all those three things to the table are the people who should be leading the charge for your Internet business. One of the common mistakes that you want to avoid is putting your Internet business into the hands of a technical genius who knows nothing about your industry or the way you sell products.

The specific kind of professionals that you choose will depend on step one—on what you've decided you want to do on the Internet. And with this in mind, there's a specific question that you'll want to think about—one that relates to the composition of your Internet team. Do you want the Internet channel to be a autonomous profit center, or to serve in a complementary role for an existing profit center? There may be good arguments for both options, but your digital strategy will only work if you think them out in advance.

One reason to think about autonomy is the measurement factor. Your Internet group may chiefly enhance what your product people or marketing people are doing, but to the extent that you can set it up as a freestanding profit center, it's easier for them to have an incentive to grow something. And that something may or may not be online transaction revenues. The incentive may be tied to leads that are generated through the Internet and then referred to sales and service for closing and follow-up. This is an important strategy to keep in mind if your product or service—gaskets or rubber tubing, for example—isn't particularly well suited to direct Internet sales.

Step Three: Establish Partnerships

Step two indicates that in drafting a digital strategy, you cannot simply decide to outsource everything. Somebody on board the ship has to keep watch, too. But the flip side of this principle is just as important. You can't establish a cyberpresence without outside help. Finding appropriate partners is critical to your success. We've made this point throughout the book with regard to conventional business partners—the kind of alliances that our company has, for example, with Compaq and Charles Schwab. But it's also important to align yourself with solid technical partners; that is, the network professionals who will help you "build the skyscraper."

Unless you're a computer manufacturer, for example, you won't be building your own Net-enabled computers. That's obvious enough. But in addition, you're probably not going to do all of your in-house design, and you probably won't physically run the servers for your Internet site. On the service provider end, you're going to need *design partners* because to consumers the appearance of your Web site is enormously important. So just as you have architects who build your physical stores and advertising agents to design your ad presence on TV, you will have partners to help you design each page's appearance as well as the "navigability" from page to page.

You will also need *technology or networking partners* who will provide you with various kinds of bandwidth and connectivity to the Internet. These technical experts may go beyond connectivity and actually provide you with a place to run your applications. That's called the "hosting" of a Web site, and it's increasingly common, because your Web site, whatever its appearance, should have a fairly predictable load. That load can be more effectively managed in a place where people are monitoring usage on a twenty-four/seven basis. That's an important component of what Internet service providers do. The downside here is that, with a hosted site, making page design changes can sometimes take a little longer than if the application were running on your own in-house server.

The other partners you might have in place are actually developed partners. They are the companies who produce the software applications that your company may be running on its Web site, and these applications will be integrated by *integration partners,* who are often very closely allied with the design partners. An example would be a stock price chart, showing your company's activity over the past several quarters. Another example would be the product configurator that enables your customers to order specific solutions online. Although neither one is your Web site in its totality, both may be essential components of your online personality, and so they need to be visually integrated to your company identity.

In this regard, it's fascinating to realize that, in this second generation of Web capability, you don't necessarily have to run your own software, or even have someone host software that you buy for your use. You can actually just point to someone else's Web site, and that Web site can take on the look and feel of your own. The major search engines began to do this a while ago, for major companies like Disney and NBC.

These companies were interested in having search capability integrated into their sites, and rather than running their own search engines, they arranged to piggyback, in a way, onto the existing engines—especially Lycos and Excite—so that, when a user goes to the "Search" function on the Disney site, he or she is using a major search engine, but it's visually designed as if he's still in the Disney universe. It's a kind of back engineering customization of a hyperlink. You can get the capability of a Lycos, but in your own custom package. It's an exciting capability that will become increasingly common.

That's a quick walk-through of the major partners that you need to consider bringing into the loop as you put together a business presence on the Internet. The nuts and bolts of actually doing that are discussed in the next chapter. But let's assume that you and your partners have already done that, or are in the process of doing it, of rolling it out. A fourth step to consider, before the actual roll-out, is to think about collecting all your data in a single repository.

Step Four: Coordinate Your Data

The Internet, by definition, is highly distributed. That's true on the macro level of global networking, in the sense that there are multiple backbones and no real center. It's also true in terms of individual businesses, because the applications that you need to run an E-business may not all be operating from the same physical place. You may have some applications that you host yourself, others that are hosted at your ISP, and even some that live at a third Internet site, like the "Disneyfied" version of Lycos that we've just described. Even more significantly, these various applications, wherever they "live" in physical space, may actually belong to different "language communities," in that they are designed to represent data in mutually unintelligible ways. If you want your applications to talk to one another, this can be a headache.

The solution, which is on the near horizon, is a central repository. The term is a little misleading, because in everyday speech the word "repository" suggests a physical location, like a warehouse or library. In cybertalk, the meaning is somewhat more subtle. When Internet experts speak about a single repository, this doesn't mean a single mainframe the size of Kansas. It means the writing of your applications in such a way that identical information is identically represented, wherever you happen to find it across your Internet presence. It's this type of identical, consistent representation that allows you to get at data from multiple perspectives and be confident that the processing will be always the same.

As sensible as this sounds, it's not common practice today, except in the most sophisticated companies. Part of the reason is proprietary warfare among software suppliers and ISPs, and part of it is the absence, so far, of a single data standard—a problem that we mentioned briefly in Chapter 2. With the acceptance of XML, this may be solved, but in the meantime, we strongly recommend that, within your own operations, you aim for uniform representation among all your databases. Achieving that will enable you to modernize your system quickly as new technologies become available, as opposed to having to referee an ongoing wrestling match among the search engines, your service providers, and your own in-house team.

For the foreseeable future, this may still be a battle, because individual repositories across the Internet are dedicated to maintaining their proprietary edge and collecting and storing customer information separately. Think of how useful it might be to you, for example, to gain access to Amazon.com's customer database— or Yahoo!'s. That's not going to happen tomorrow, and it won't come free. But for E-business to prosper in a distributed universe, there has eventually got to be a move toward a single-language solution. This, by the way, this is why PlanetAll is going to be such a valuable business. They are already providing the necessary groundwork for bringing it all together.

Step Five: Measure the Effectiveness

Once your data is all in place and your Web site (or nongraphical application) is up and running, you'll need to check the effectiveness of what you've rolled out. By "effectiveness," we mean effectiveness against your competition, and this isn't always as obvious as it may seem. We've seen how the Internet changes many traditional business rules. One of these changes relates to the very definition of "competitor."

For example, there are a number of companies that produce a whole variety of CD-ROMs aimed at the home improvement and home entertainment markets. There's a genealogy product that helps you build a family tree, a carpentry tool that shows you how to put up closet shelves, a landscaping tool that enables you to plot out your backyard garden, color coordinating your flower beds right on the screen. For a while, this has been an extremely popular example of niche marketing—visually pleasing applications that are widely available, at points of sale ranging from Egghead to Office Depot to Target—all competing with one another, off-line.

With the rise of Internet business, that is changing. With the Internet, if you're interested in this kind of do-it-yourself advice, you might not want to pick it up off the shelf. You might go instead to a building supplier's Web site, where you can download a landscaping tool for free, and where the supplier is happy to have you do that because it means you're likely to be coming into one of its many outlets to purchase the tools that you need to complete the project.

So you no longer pay forty dollars to a software developer. You pay forty dollars for a rake, a shovel, ten bags of soil, and a couple of potted plants, to the supplier, which provided you with the landscaping applications for free. Which means that, if you're the CD-ROM vendor, you've got a new competitor. Now it's not just *Home & Garden* magazine releasing its own CD, but a broad range of garden outlets, who can attract your customers by giving away what you once sold them.

It can work from the other direction, too. The building supplier may think of its competition as dozens of mom-and-pop hardware stores around the country, vying with their individual outlets for local business. But today, national competition may include a single mom-and-pop business in Twin Forks, Idaho, that has leveraged the Web into a visibility that challenges the giants. Or a mail-order catalog company like Smith and Hawken.

The model established by mail order, in fact, is quite relevant. What the mail-order companies did was to challenge the traditional assumption that you had to have a physical store to draw in customers. That paper-flipping model was the predecessor of the Net. The Net provides the next level of nontraditional competition, and it has the capability, because of its speed and its efficiency, to change the playing field. That's why, as you're going online, you've got to survey that field carefully, to see how you're doing competitively against emerging new players.

That's the big picture that you need to know to roll it all out. But the implementation, naturally, is also detail driven—it's a matter of individual decisions about a thousand nuts and bolts. If you're going to be personally involved in making these decisions, if you're going to be working directly with your design and network partners, or if you just want a ground's-eye view of the parameters involved, we recommend that you read the following chapter. If these areas are not your concern, you can skip to Chapter 12, where we underline the point that going digital is mission-critical.

Chapter 11

Rolling It Out II

Nuts and Bolts

The previous chapter defined in broad terms the technical requirements for establishing an E-business presence. For most large companies—including most Siebel customers—the mechanics of turning this blueprint into a reality will be handled in-house by sophisticated IT departments. If you have that kind of in-house capability, and are confident in your people's ability to create the responsiveness we've just described, you may not need the specifics that we're going to describe in this chapter. You may want to fast-forward through it or go directly to Chapter 12.

If, on the other hand, you're a smaller operation and you expect to rely on outsourcing to implement your E-business solution, this chapter will be a valuable guide for turning theory into practice. In it we discuss the nuts and bolts of actually implementing an online business, give practical advice for making your Web site a productive sales and marketing channel, and suggest the expertise that you should look for in your technology professionals.

Whatever your company's size and whatever choices you decide to make regarding internal versus external solutions, there are five concrete steps that your company needs to follow to make any online presence a working reality. They are:

- Finding an Internet service provider
- Registering a domain name
- Developing the Web site
- Managing the site
- Measuring its effectiveness

The last step implies a question that you should ask yourself even before you find a service provider. To test for effectiveness, you've got to know what "effective" means. So begin by asking yourself, realistically, what goals you expect to accomplish by having a Web site. What do you expect an online presence to perform for your company? The answer may be online sales, brand building, better communication with your customers, or some combination of these. Whatever your expectations, be sure that they're clearly understood by everyone in your company who might have contact with the online customer stream.

We recommend following the advice of Bill Kilday, who is president of the Web consultancy Modem-Operandi Interactive *(www.m-o.net)*. "Too many companies," Bill says, "are asking what they can do to fit themselves to the Web. Instead, what you should be asking is how the Web can fit your company, how it can help you improve your processes, how it can help you do better what you're already doing. Focus on current communication going on between you, your customers, and your suppliers and then figure out how the Web can help you improve that communication."

Focusing on the customer stream from the start will help you avoid the problem of neglecting or mismanaging it, and it will also give you a handle on budget requirements. Web site roll-out costs can be as low as a couple of hundred dollars, for an online billboard, and they can run into the hundreds of thousands of dollars for an integrated, multifunctional commerce site. Decide up front what commitment you're ready to make to E-business, and what ROI you expect that commitment to deliver.

Once you're clear on this score, your company is ready to look for an ISP.

Step One: Finding an ISP

Locating an Internet service provider, or ISP, is easy. Check the Yellow Pages under "Internet" or get the Boardwatch Directory of Internet Service Providers *(www.boardwatch.com/ISP/usisp.htm)*. You'll find thousands of them out there, ranging from small local companies that provide the basics like dial-up service and e-mail, to UUNET and other giant nationals, with the capacity to host and operate huge commerce sites. They all want your business, but they're not all equally reliable—and size itself isn't necessarily a guarantee of quality. To sort out the service providers from the service pretenders, you need to interview carefully and ask pointed questions. The most critical questions relate to the potential problem areas of bandwidth availability, security, and troubleshooting.

Bandwidth. The principal issues here have to do with Net "backbones," which are the largest, trunklike networks within the Internet itself. Since even the smallest local ISP accesses the Net through one or more backbones, ask which backbone or backbones the ISP uses, how many high-speed links it has to a backbone, and how "thick" its connecting lines are to this central highway. T1 lines are good, but T3 lines are better, and as in any mission-critical application, look for redundancy. A good rule of thumb, according to one technical analyst, is that "any ISP supporting business customers should have at least three T1 or faster connections to two or more different backbones."

Ask also about the ISP's performance ("How long does an average transmission take?" and "What capacity of your bandwidth is being used?") and about that of the backbone to which it's connected. Performance tests of Internet service providers can be purchased from Keynote Systems *(www.keynote.com)* for about $500. As for backbones, be aware that they are not all created equal; you might compare the major carriers' reliability by checking out a *Boardwatch Magazine* study. Available online at *www. boardwatch.com/isp/fall1997/measure.html,* it found that the best-performing backbone in the United States was run by relatively small Savvis Communications *(www.savvis.com),* which has moved away from the overloaded public access lines (like MAE-West and MAE-East) to construct "private peering" alliances with other small networks.

Security. Since your ISP will serve as a conduit for your company's data, you'll want to know how careful they will be about protecting it. So ask: "What are the security measures that you have in place to ensure that only my authorized representatives see my data?" The answer should explain the provider's use of firewalls, encryption, user IDs and passwords, secure network cables, and even such "obvious" protections as locked doors and security guards. Be sure that the ISP has provisions for securing its network not only from outside hackers but also from its own employees. Getting clear answers about this is essential to your peace of mind, so if the answers don't make you feel confident, look somewhere else.

This is especially important if the service provider is also functioning as a Web site "host," that is, if the "server" computer that will interact with your company's "client" computers is physically housed at the ISP location. If the server is at your company, you can watch it yourself, and many companies house their own servers for precisely that reason. If it's more convenient to put it on somebody else's premises, fine. But be sure you know who's watching it there, and how. The same principle applies if your server sits on a "Web hoster" computer—one of the emerging alternatives to ISP siting.

Troubleshooting. With the best performance and redundancy in the world, problems still occur: In the words of an industry slogan, "Downtime happens." What you want from a service provider is not the guarantee that it will never happen to you (anybody who tells you that is deluded or lying), but the assurance that, when it does, it will be dealt with aggressively. So ask the following questions before you sign on:

- "Do you have twenty-four/seven human assistance? Can I talk to a technical support person at three in the morning? How long will it take me to get him or her on the line?"

- "What alternate methods of contact do you make available? Can I reach you through phone, e-mail, and the Web?"
- "What's your average turnaround time for a service call?"
- "What's your service response process? What happens first, second, and third, when a customer has a problem? How much time elapses between one attempted solution and the next escalated one?"

Get references, too. If somebody boasts about a one-hour troubleshooting average but has no customers who can verify it, don't scratch your head—find somebody else. The "S" in ISP stands for "service." If that's what your company is paying for, demand that you get it.

Trust your instincts. Consider the sunglass maker Gargoyles. Shopping for an ISP a few years ago, the company's systems analyst, Dominic Lindauer, looked at everything from the national telcos to local providers with significantly lower prices. One of the telcos bragged that its server was in an old missile silo, so that, even in a nuclear strike, it would keep running. "If there were a nuclear strike," Lindauer mused, "I don't think I'd need to check our Web site to see if new orders were taken." Others offered free equipment or service packages that sounded good in the abstract but that were irrelevant to Gargoyles' business. The lower-bid ISPs had phenomenal discounts, but when Lindauer expressed concerns about their financial stability, they gave him "attitude" rather than information.

He settled on Epoch Internet, even though its price was higher, because their willingness to prove their reliability eased his mind. A test call to their tech support line got him solid responses, they brought in "a ton of people" to educate him about firewalls, and they agreed to a service agreement that allowed Gargoyles to terminate the association if Internet connections were broken for more than forty-eight hours. It was comfort level, not bells and whistles, that made the difference.

Now, you may want some bells and whistles. Internet service providers will offer you lots of technical extras, from remote access capability to spam protection, and depending on your needs and your budget, you may want to consider them. But don't confuse these services with basic reliability.

Step Two: Registering Your Name

If you're going to be doing business over the Internet, there are two places that you must register your company name. One is with a central URL registry, which for the past few years has been overseen jointly by the Network Information Center, Network Solutions Inc., and the National Science Foundation; for a $100 fee, you can register with this "InterNIC" body online at *rs. internic.net/reg*. The other is with the Web's own directories, or search engines, which route user inquiries to the appropriate URLs. These two registrations work symbiotically; one without the other is basically useless.

InterNIC registration. This is also known as URL registration, for "universal resource locator," and "domain name registration." Domains are the suffixes that follow a company's Web site name in a URL address, the most common one in E-business being ".com," for "commercial." Other common domains—they're actually known as top-level domains, or TLDs—include .net ("networks"), .edu ("educational"), and .org ("organizations"). A complete company address thus includes the World Wide Web prefix, the company name, and the suffix. For our company, it's *www.siebel.com*. If you want to reach the company Web page, that's what you type. If you want to e-mail an individual within the company, you usually give the person's Web name at the company.

So, when you register a domain name, what you're really registering is the company name—or, rather, the name that you go by on the World Wide Web. That sounds straightforward, but because InterNIC follows a first-come, first-served rule, your company name may already have been spoken for, and you will have to devise a logical or catchy alternative. You can use any name you want that hasn't already been taken. Be aware that, with nearly 1 million new names being registered each year, you might not be officially registered for a month or so. Be aware, too, that Network Solution's virtual control over domain names is now being challenged by competitors. Under emerging protocols, analysts believe, competition for registry rights will soon be heating up, especially with the establishment of a revised naming system that is to include new, generic domain names (so-called gTLDs) like .firm, .arts, and .shop.

Search engine registration. Search engine registration is optional, but you'd be well advised to do it. When you register with Yahoo!, Excite, AltaVista, or another search engine, you submit a company description and some keywords to help identify your business focus. The search engine uses these keywords to understand what you do, and to route users who submit matching keywords to your company Web site. Without that routing process, you're just floating in cyberspace.

This is how it's supposed to work, anyway. In fact, Yahoo! and the other directories are often more seriously backed up than InterNIC, meaning that your request for routing may be delayed, and sometimes even lost. Modem-Operandi's Bill Kilday calls the search engine registration process "a black hole of mystery." "It may take them six months to get you in, or it may never happen," he says. "That's why the no-fee services are now meeting fee-based competition. At one new search engine, Goto.com, you pay for your listing—actually, bid on it. You bid for a higher placement, so when your description comes up, you're not number 304 out of 305."

Goto.com isn't alone. AltaVista is moving toward the same strategy, with the recent introduction of a "Real Name" search process. In partnership with Centraal Corporation, AltaVista now maintains a database of a half million keywords and phrases, any of which a company can associate with its site for an annual fee of forty dollars. The association pulls that site out of the morass of possible hits and places it, with other Real Name hits, at the top of the search results. So, for example, someone interested in reading about the new Beetle would "immediately find a Volkswagen site, rather than having to scroll through pages of entomological references first." It's an inexpensive way of standing apart from the pack, and a welcome simplification for the data-drenched surfer.

Step Three: Selecting a Web Developer

The third step is to select a person or a company who can actually "construct" your Web site and get it online. Some large companies do this in-house, but for most small and mid-size firms, the solution is outsourcing. Check the Yellow Pages again, or the Web itself. Look under "Internet Solutions" or "Web Site Development."

The usual term for someone who sets up your Web pages is web designer, but as anybody who has suffered through an artsy but clunky site can tell you, "well designed" isn't necessarily synonymous with "effective." A good Web site is both. But to get both, you may have to look to companies that provide a total package, not just the colors and squiggles for which Web designers are famous.

"I look for three things in a Web developer," says Holt Rinehart and Winston marketing VP Ted Finch. "A good eye, technical ability, and marketing savvy. The first gives you taste, which is hard to define but easy to recognize when you've got it. The second means the person can translate an inner vision into a physical counterpart—and do the technical adjustments that you may need on the fly. The third, marketing savvy, is absolutely essential. If the basic purpose of the site is to promote your business, it has got to be handled by someone who appreciates that fact."

Bill Kilday, who has worked with various companies on Web site development, agrees. "Designers and technologists have completely different skill sets," he says. "You need both, but you're not necessarily going to find them in the same person. You've got to bring the artists together with the people who know what hardware and software you need. Whether you're getting it done in house or at your ISP or through a third party, that fusion is essential. A Web developer does design *and* technology."

The type of advice and assistance a good developer can provide you will vary depending on your budget, how elaborate you want the site to be, and its purpose. At the very least, he or she should help you set up attractive displays of the following information:

- Your company name and logo
- A description of what you do and how you came to do it; that is, your business model, your mission, and a brief company history
- An identification of senior management, preferably with photos to personalize who you are
- A list of your products or services, along with their prices if you're planning to sell them online
- Contact information for customers or business partners, including one-click instructions for sending you e-mail
- Evidence of your success, including references, press releases, or news reports
- A table of contents and/or index to what's on the site, along with easily navigable links from one page to another
- A prominently displayed announcement of your privacy policy, to reassure customers you won't be divulging their personal information

If you're rolling out a full-fledged commerce site, you'll also want recommendations about hardware and software options (including "shopping cart" capabilities), information on how to ensure the distinction between your "private" and "public" Web pages, and help with setting up the necessary order and billing procedures with delivery partners and credit card transaction authorities. With all the bells and whistles in the world, a good commerce site only runs smoothly if these essential pieces are put in place correctly at the outset. A good developer makes you confident that this is being done.

Many sites also include an FAQ, or "frequently asked questions," feature. These are useful if carefully designed, but problematic if they're not well thought out. If you think you want an FAQ option, find out first which really are the frequently asked questions in your market space. Ask the people who know—your customer service people and call center agents—and discuss their input with your Web developer. You'll probably find out that there are fewer FAQs than you imagined, and that most of them can be stated generally. "What are your color options?" might be an FAQ. "Can I get the Model 24 in magenta?" isn't.

In working with a Web developer, you'll also want to ask about links. This part of overall page design is what enables your customers to navigate easily not only from page to page within your Web site, but also from your Web site to related sites—for example, those of your business partners. This, too, requires technology and design working together.

Finally, in choosing a developer, use the same common sense that you would in choosing an ISP, a Web hoster, or any other business partner. Ask the tough questions, demand clear answers, and look at the evidence. The evidence, with Web developers, is their previous work, the sites that they have designed for other business clients. You give your customers references. Get the same thing from any developer you're considering.

Ask for the URL of a showcase account and spend some time

there. If you find the experience pleasant, informative, and inter-active, then this developer is one that you'll want to consider. If you find his showcase site slow, confusing, or in any way unap-pealing to you, look for someone else. The look and feel of a Web site is a company's electronic lobby. If you don't feel good being there, neither will your customers.

And don't be dazzled by cosmetics at the expense of practical-ity. This is an important, though counterintuitive, point that bears some elaboration.

There are two hypothetical extremes in Web page design. At one extreme is useful but boring. At the other extreme the site is a visual delight, but it doesn't really work. Avoid both extremes. Aim for the kind of balance found on a Web page that the design firm Web Mania! produced for an Oklahoma catalog site called The Apple Cart. This online store is the brainchild of a high school math teacher who, in 1996, decided to go into business for herself. After a year of running a small shop, she moved to the In-ternet, so as "not to miss out on this new frontier," and has since then done so well with her apple-motif merchandise that she is considering having to invest in a larger warehouse.

The Apple Cart site is lean and clean. The opening page fea-tures a company description, a display of the credit cards ac-cepted, instructions for e-mailing the company, a reminder to bookmark the page, links to brief comments on company history and security practices, a couple of banner ads, a notice of a Web design award, and a button with the quiet announcement "Enter the Store." Once inside the store, customers find full-color pho-tographs of the company's products, with ordering instructions. The apple logo is prominently displayed, but it doesn't flash or gyrate—it's just there. The design, in short, makes the shopping experience more enjoyable, rather than calling attention to its own ingenuity.

Your site should be pleasing to the eye. But if you sink all your R&D money into visual bells and whistles, you risk undermining the advantages of having a site at all. That's not because the multicolored kaleidoscope that your Web designer thought was so attractive actually gets in the way of your business message (although it may). It's because elaborate graphics put a severe strain on bandwidth capacity, and downloading them takes infinitely longer than downloading text. Think of the "three-second rule" as a complement to the three-click rule: If your customers aren't seeing something after three seconds, you may be testing their patience and risking an attack of clickitis. The best advice is to go for attractive, not flashy.

You will get other advice. The Internet, like the computer industry, is pulsing with technophiles who believe that if a program can be written, then by God it should be, and if a page can be designed in twenty colors, then color away. These people are on every silicon street corner, and you might even want to hire some of them. We have. They can be highly productive employees and fascinating friends. Just don't ask them to design your Web site.

Step Four: Managing the Site

Once your Web site is up, you've got to manage it. Part of that is getting people to visit it—an advertising task. Another part is monitoring the site to be sure that it's consistently up-to-date, running smoothly, and attracting the quantity and quality of visitors you want. To perform those functions, companies typically employ a "Webmaster."

In spite of the term's evocation of Dungeons and Dragons, Webmasters' wizardry actually has less to do with magic than with marketing acumen. They have to display the same combination of technical and artistic competence that you want from a Web developer, and in fact many developers also function as Webmasters. But whereas Web site development delivers a finished product, Webmastering is an ongoing process, a task whose very definition is continual monitoring. In addition, Webmasters, while they may work on an outsource basis, are increasingly being hired to work in-house, either under their own budget or as part of an IT department.

The "typical" Webmaster today, according to a survey done by the research firm CustomerSat.com, is a self-taught male in his mid-thirties. Responsible for a site with roughly 100 megabytes of content, he earns a high-forties salary, oversees a staff of three or four, and works with a budget of $100,000 or more. Accounting for that average are companies that spend less than $10,000 on their sites and companies that may budget $1 million or more. The trend is up, too. Between 1996 and 1998, the percentage of firms that spent between $100,000 and more than a million on their sites rose from just under 19 percent to nearly 31 percent. Webmasters are managing increasingly hefty IT budgets.

They're also leveraging a growing suite of Web tools, from basic construction or "authoring" applications like HomeSite, to design tools like FrontPage and Fusion, to traffic analysis tools like WebTrends, to comprehensive management tools like Vignette. These tools are bringing new complexities and new possibilities into the electronic commerce space, and a good Webmaster keeps on top of such developments. We're way past the point where a Webmaster was the tie-dyed Wunderkind in the back room whose idea of design was some "way cool" colors. There's nothing wrong with color. But the corporate Webmaster today is, literally, all business.

Which means an equal attention to new technology and to market trends. Many companies point to this in their job descriptions. The buzz may be that they're looking to hire a Webmaster. But the official title may be "online marketing manager." Whether part of the IT department or not, the Webmaster may well report to the VP of marketing, and will be chiefly responsible for enhancing that function. Again, technology is important, but it's not about technology. It's about communicating with your customers and securing your markets.

As you look for a qualified Webmaster, whether the function is in-house or outsourced, consider the general duties that you expect the person to perform. These will begin with the regular updating of your company home page to ensure that it reflects the latest press releases, news stories, and promotions. You may want the Webmaster to design and implement promotions himself or herself, as a way of encouraging and amplifying traffic to your site. He or she should be responsible for maintaining any databases to which your customers or business partners will have online access. And certainly he should meticulously monitor the major Web search engines, to be sure that you are properly referenced in their keyword databases.

Depending on your business, there may be further duties that you would reasonably expect of a Webmaster, from maintaining marketing links to posting research, from updating product comparisons to answering customer queries. Whatever the specifics, keep the marketing function in mind. Notice the focus of the following job description from a trade paper advertisement for an online marketing manager:

> The ideal candidate is market savvy and understands the strategic importance of an effective marketing Web site. He/she can program effectively in HTML, Java, and other needed disciplines, and has excellent graphical taste, with either the capability to design or the eye to approve designs that match the corporate image. In addition, this person is service oriented and understands that his/her role will be in servicing the online needs of the marketing department and in proactively marketing, developing, and improving the Web site. . . . As keeper of the site, this person is highly trusted and is a team player.

"Keeper" of the site. That's a common term, as is "owner" of the site. Both of them illustrate the importance of the Webmaster function. As your company's principal pathway into the virtual marketplace, your Web site must be managed with meticulous zeal. It's the role of the company Webmaster to ensure that this happens.

Step Five: Measuring Effectiveness

Given the major investment that most Web sites entail, it's only common sense to measure the return. The simplest way to do this is by counting hard figures, from number of dollars transacted (or saved) to number of visitors. Companies that measure in this way have found, in many cases, that the returns from a well-managed Web site can be quite phenomenal.

Much of the return can be traced to operating cost savings. In 1997, Cisco's site saved the company an estimated $363 million in technical, marketing, and distribution costs, a lot of that from the automation of its customer service. Not bad for an initial outlay of $50 million and an annual Web site budget of only $10 million. Other large firms have seen comparable ROIs, especially through the implementation of corporate intranets. When International Data Corporation surveyed seven E-business leaders—including Lockheed Martin, Deere & Company, and Booz, Allen & Hamilton—they found that six of the seven had ROIs of 1,000 percent or more.

Of course, returns like these are predicated on a heavy initial investment, and so are those that can be measured in terms of "hits." The CustomerSat.com survey we mentioned earlier found a direct correlation between site budget and daily traffic. Among organizations that spent less than $10,000 on their sites, 60 percent saw 100 or fewer visitors a day. When the investments rose to between $50,000 and $100,000, the traffic rose to between 100 and 1000 daily visits, and the handful of companies that committed $1 million or more to their sites drew daily rates that averaged one visitor per dollar. Given that the average 800 call can cost you much more than that, it seems that the more you invest, the more you may save.

But money is only one measure of a site's success. You can have a successful site that generates little revenue, so long as it answers the purpose for which it was designed. Maybe that purpose is brand recognition, or the enhancement of customer confidence, or online support of your brick-and-mortar outlets. What you hope to get out of the site determines how you'll measure its success.

Ticketmaster, for example, recently sued its business partner Microsoft for routing ticket buyers to a Ticketmaster site. It wasn't as crazy as it sounds because, as Ticketmaster saw it, a principal purpose of its site was to sell advertising space, and the purchasing page within that site to which Microsoft was routing customers bypassed ads that were visible on the "correct" way in. So Ticketmaster lost ad exposure every time it sold a ticket. The lesson is that you measure return by how well it covers your investment, however your company chooses to define that.

One element in measuring that investment is tracking your traffic. This means more than keeping a visitor log. All a visitor log tells you is how many people have walked in to your electronic lobby. That's not really very helpful in planning a customer strategy, a product mix, or the look of your Web site itself. It's just as important to know what they do once they're "inside."

Ted Finch, vice president of marketing for the schoolbook publisher Holt, Rinehart and Winston *(www.hrw.com)*, recommends a tracking system based on a merchandising model, where store managers use a "Plan-o-Gram" to regulate traffic flow. "It's a representation," Finch explains, "of an adjustable floor plan. In a WalMart or a Toys R Us, you get profits inch by inch, so you want to maximize the revenue you are getting from any given aisle, any given shelf in that aisle, and any section of that shelf. You do that by measuring the traffic at all those levels, and then adjusting the layout of the store to create better returns. Higher profit is the direct result of optimal routing.

"In a physical store, you use physical structures to shift the traffic patterns. Toys R Us arranges its aisles so that, even if you're just popping in for a box of diapers, you've got to walk past the impulse items, which are placed at kid level. If WalMart is overstocked on garden supplies, that inventory is moved to a high-traffic lane.

"You use the same routing principles in designing a Web site. Every server these days has statistical software that can tell you where your visitors are clicking, page by page. So you can get a very precise picture of how your site is being navigated. If your customers aren't going where you want them to go, you do exactly what WalMart or Toys R Us does: You rearrange your site plan until they go where you intend."

You don't need to be a programming whiz to do this rearranging. There are some very user-friendly, very intuitive page-design programs out there that anyone can use just as easily as a merchandiser's Plan-o-Gram.

"A lot of people use Adobe PageMill," says Finch. "Others use programs like NetObjects Fusion. It displays your entire site in a multitiered diagram, with the starting page buttons at the top and the links underneath, so you get a bird's-eye take on the floor plan and the traffic flow. Rearranging the flow is just drag-and-drop, and you can do that as often as you want, in any number of combinations, so that the site is reflective of what you want it to do."

What *you* want it to do. That's crucial, and since it varies from company to company, sometimes day to day, your refinement of the electronic floor plan should vary, too. For example, if you're running a promotion on a brand-new product, you shouldn't tuck that information away in a third-tier "Products" box: Highlight the special on your opening page. Or, if you use your Web site to

direct your customers to retail outlets but nobody is actually clicking on your outlet directory, then you'll probably need to consider
some design modifications. Maybe the locator link isn't prominently enough displayed. Maybe it needs a catchier or more descriptive title. Maybe it needs to be positioned on every page.

Whatever modifications you decide on, getting customers to
click on your home page is only step one. To get them into the
"aisles," you should track their movements. And make it easy for
them to go where you want them to.

A Final Word: Remembering the Customer

We've stressed that your Web site should do what you want it to
do, but what that really means—or should mean—is that it
should do for your customers what *they* want it to. Your plans for
the site and your customers' plans had better be similar, because
it's your customers (and your business partners) who will be using
the site, and if it doesn't make sense to them, you can forget about
returns—in both senses of that word. That's why ongoing site
measurement should enlist customer feedback and take it into account in improving the experience.

Take a tip from Millipore Corporation, a $600 million manu-
facturer of purification products. When they conducted an online
survey of their Web site a couple of years ago, they found that
their customers weren't terribly excited about making online payments; what they really wanted was the ability to track pending
orders. So Millipore directed its systems analysts to add that
functionality. Now customers can enter an order number on the
Web site, and the system will check it against a file that is updated

every three hours. Tom Anderson, the company's director of corporate communications, explains the philosophy simply: "We ask what our customers want and then we give it to them."

Here's how another Web marketer assesses the importance of customer input:

> Successful customer service always means looking at your products, your company, and your customer service methods through your customers' eyes. The customer doesn't care if your company is organized by product line, business unit, or spheres of political influence. The customer wants his or her question answered or problem solved.
>
> The most important task for a customer service Web builder to undertake is figuring out what the customer will want to see, want to ask, and want to get out of the experience. It may well be worth the effort to ask them directly, "If you were able to do business with us via our Web site, what sort of functionality would you like to see?"

It's not only worth the effort. It's essential to the effort. The best Web sites now running, whether public or private, are effective because they are responsive to customer input. That's a lesson of business in general, after all. Why wouldn't it be a lesson of online marketing?

Rolling your Web site out is a complex process—so complex that sometimes, when a company has finally accomplished it, the owners of the site lean back and say, "Whew! Glad that's over." That's an understandable reaction, but it can be deadly. Getting your Web site up and rolling gets you in the game. Keeping you there is a process that never ends.

Chapter 12

Mission Critical

Business activity on the Internet is barely five years old, yet in that short span of time it has grown from a smattering of electronic storefronts to a massive infrastructure, planetary in its reach and unparalleled in human history for its ability to rationalize and intensify commercial enterprise. Five years, and the number of business Web sites is already doubling every two months. Shopping from a computer has become a welcome option for half the computer-owning population, and a single on-line leader, Cisco Systems, is looking toward $4 billion in annual revenues. In the first five years of E-business, we've come a long way.

But that five years represents merely the first generation. It's been an exciting and productive one, to be sure, but nothing compared to what succeeding generations will achieve. Amazon.com's leader Jeff Bezos has it right when he says we're still in the Kitty Hawk era of electronic business. The next generation will be simply extraordinary, as the vast potential of Internet commerce begins to be realized, and as we move incrementally closer to a fully connected world. The Internet has the ability to transform the planet, and we are already seeing the beginnings of that transformation.

Five years, and already new software solutions for E-business are coming on to the market every week, making it possible to set up a virtual shop within a few days. Capital investment in E-business infrastructure is going through the roof, as more and more companies bet on commercial applications as their unavoidable destiny. More and more companies are being founded to address the issues of E-business, and more and more are failing, as the virtual landscape changes daily before our eyes.

We are at a critical juncture today. Five years from now, as we come to the end of the first decade of E-business, we may well identify 1998 as the critical "takeoff" moment for this new commercial paradigm. That was the year in which we reached a critical mass of infrastructure that provided (1) improved Net access, (2) better security, and (3) streamlined electronic payment systems. As a result, almost every measure of E-business potential began to accelerate then. Venture capital spending for Internet companies was at a historic high, and rising fast. Company IT spending on intranet/extranet projects broke records, and E-business sites began to show real profits. In 1998 we experienced the first "kick" in an exponential E-business curve.

To what heights will that curve bring us in the next five years? In this book we've provided some preliminary answers to that question. We've shown how cyber rules have already transformed the business landscape and how the revolutionary power of Internet connectivity is enhancing global enterprise, mass customization, and customer service. We've described the rich potential of "para-enterprises" and looked ahead to the very near future, when software agents will drive a uniquely "intelligent" commercial explosion. But what about the longer view? What will E-business look like a decade, or two decades, from now?

Predictions get increasingly fuzzy as you get farther out, but one thing seems clear. The trip from "here," where most online buying and selling is being done through Web catalogs, to "there," a not-so-distant future where most buying and selling transactions will be automated and occur over the medium of the Internet, will very likely be a bumpy ride. It will make a lot of people very rich, but it will also result in casualties along the way. And some of those casualties may transform the face of the economy.

It has been estimated, for example, that if the Internet subsumes even as little as 15 percent of normal commerce (this does not include existing electronic transactions such as online banking or ATMs), we will see massive failures of conventional local businesses, whose high overhead and lack of variety will render them noncompetitive. And this represents only the first shifts toward a new world economy. In another twenty or thirty years, it may be that the rules of commerce (an institution that has served us for thousands of years) will undergo a fundamental redefinition, as the Internet becomes more and more capable of supporting a real-time, electronic connection between every individual and every business in the world. In the process thousands, perhaps millions, will be put out of work—even as greater opportunities beckon to the survivors.

Once E-business achieves critical mass, we will have a single, universal "commerce engine" in place. Powering the world's transactions, it will purr with efficiency and permeate the electronic landscape. New companies, free from the current wrangling over shared standards, will be able to focus on building end-user value; that is, on improving the quality of their customers' lives. Opportunities will abound. So will risks. And everything will be connected—more so than ever.

How will companies survive in this superconnected world? And how can your company ensure that, when it arrives, you'll still be among the players who are sitting at the table? Three suggestions:

First, become technoliterate. In this book, we've provided a sketch of the technological options that every contender in the digital universe ought to be familiar with. Use it as a springboard to further research. Even if you're too small a firm to have an IT department, make the sharpening of your IT *function* a business priority.

Within the next ten years at the most, a deep competitive divide will become established between a technological elite and everybody else. That divide is already emerging at the workforce level, and it also explains why the world's business leaders are in the high-tech arena. If you want to be a player in the twenty-first century, you've got to become comfortable with the language of digital commerce.

This doesn't mean that everybody in your company, from the

CEO on down, has to speak computerese like a Silicon Valley native. It does mean that the management of your company's information systems must be recognized across the board as mission critical. And that keeping up with developments in this warp-speed world is the designated responsibility of a senior manager.

Second, be patient. As we move toward the fully connected future, it may sometimes seem that it is taking forever to provide sufficient bandwidth to realize a business goal, or that the building of a truly secure firewall is a hopeless task. But we're getting closer to those goals every day, and when they are finally achieved, the opportunities will be endless. The infrastructure—the Internet's immense grid of wires—is developing gradually, like television did in the early 1950s. It will slowly but inexorably begin to provide more bandwidth, more power, more reliability, more security, more privacy—and the most extensive business opportunities in world history.

Third, and most important, remember your customers. Remember Bill Kilday's acute observation about Web site development: Success will come to those who ask not "How can I make a killing off the World Wide Web?" but "How can the Web help me serve my customers better?" Whatever the technofuture ends up looking like, you've got to do whatever it takes to keep your customers successful. Without that commitment, even a T3 line is a dull tool. With it, you can make any technology work to your advantage.

It's been an exciting five years, this first generation, but the second five is promising to be even better. Whether you're online already or still in the planning stage, we hope that this book has given you a glimpse of the stunning possibilities that await us on a not-at-all distant horizon. The E-business train is hurtling toward that horizon at amazing speed. Whether or not you think that you're prepared for the ride, that train is moving in the direction of business's future.

In explaining why becoming Internet-compliant is mission critical, industry consultant Jim Dickie puts it well: "It's not easy, it's not cheap, and it's not optional." That is a sobering lesson, but an exciting one. If you're ready to take it to heart—welcome aboard.

Notes

We're grateful to the print and World Wide Web sources cited below and also to the following individuals who agreed to be interviewed: Warren Adams, president and cofounder of PlanetAll; Mike Betzer, vice-president of information technology for MCI-Worldcom; Ted Finch, vice-president of marketing for Holt, Rinehart and Winston; Bill Kilday, president of Modem-Operandi Interactive; Joseph Lassiter, professor of management at the Harvard Business School; Daniel Leemon, chief strategy officer of the Charles Schwab Corporation; Salman Malik, product manager for Siebel Systems's Internet applications; Eric Schmidt, chairman and CEO of Novell Inc.; Pete Solvik, chief information officer at Cisco Systems; and John White, formerly the chief information officer at Compaq.

Introduction: The Digital Watershed

3 *Consider these statistics* Except where otherwise indicated, Internet statistics in this Introduction are drawn from the May 4, 1998, issues of "Internet Facts," at *parallaxweb.com;* CommerceNet Research Library's "Industry Statistics," at *commerce.net;* and Wylie Wong, "Commerce Study Outlines Internet Potential," in *Computer Reseller News,* May 4, 1998: 103–5.

4 *Beginning from a smidgen* Kathleen Murphy, "Venture Funds Put $1.8B into Net in 1997," *Internet World,* February 23, 1998.

6 *Here's an example* Kevin Kelly, "New Rules for the New Economy: Twelve Dependable Principles for Thriving in a Turbulent World," *Wired,* September 1997: 141–43, 186–97.

6 *Eric Schmidt* The Novell chairman was interviewed by Tad Tuleja on August 29, 1998.

8 *"Rapture of the Net"* See Cliff Barney, "Bewildered New World," *Upside,* November 1997: 108–15, 178–79.

12 *"Internots"* See Bruno Giussani, "Trying to Get Executive 'Internots' to Use the Net as a Business Tool," *CyberTimes,* July 15, 1997, at *www.nytimes.com.*

Chapter 1: The Virtual Marketplace

17 *If you looked* Mike Betzer was interviewed by Tad Tuleja on October 1, 1998.

17 *John White* The former Compaq executive was interviewed by Tad Tuleja on September 2, 1998.

19 *According to the rhetoric* See Cliff Barney, "Bewildered New World," *Upside,* November 1997: 108.

21 *"economies of scope"* B. Joseph Pine II, *Mass Customization: The*

New Frontier in Business Competition (Boston: Harvard Business School Press, 1993), 48.

21 *the new "marketspace"* The term "marketspace" was first popularized by Harvard Business School professors Jeffrey F. Rayport and John J. Sviokla in their article "Managing in the Marketspace," *Harvard Business Review,* November–December 1994: 141–50.

22 *"water cooler effect"* See Evan I. Schwartz, *Webonomics: Nine Essential Principles for Growing Your Business on the World Wide Web* (New York: Broadway Books, 1997), 15.

23 *1998 roundtable* Nelson Wang, "Ad Executives Still See Missing Pieces on Web," *Internet World,* May 18, 1998: 16.

25 *"electronic shopping mall"* For early misconceptions about retail potential, see Donna L. Hoffman and Thomas P. Novak, "Commercializing the Information Superhighway: Are We in for a Smooth Ride?" *Owen Manager* 15/2 (1994).

26 *Barron's* See "Internet Facts," at *www.parallaxweb.com.*

27 *"knowledge workers"* Peter Drucker, *Post-Capitalist Society* (New York: HarperBusiness, 1993), 83–96.

28 *"If the process was that easy"* McMahon is quoted in Paul Korzeniowski, "E-commerce on the Net a Wealth of Opportunity," *Computer Reseller News,* December 1, 1997: 83.

30 *AmeriTrade* See Sharon Machlis, "Web Businesses Spend Big on Ads," *Computerworld,* February 9, 1998: 2.

30 *"You gotta be the winner"* Walowski is quoted in James Oliver Cury, "Marketing Might," Austin/San Antonio *Computer Currents,* May 1998: 15.

30 *"That's what URL stands for"* See Eric Schmidt, "New Face of the Network," *Computer Reseller News,* December 1, 1997: 154.

30 *Eric expanded* In his August 29, 1998, conversation with Tad Tuleja.

Chapter 2: Problems and Prospects

34 *search engines only scratch* Thomas E. Weber, "Web's Vastness Foils Even Best Search Engines," *Wall Street Journal,* April 3, 1998: B1.

40 *That shift is coming* Todd Spangler, "Promising Satellite Services Emerge as Alternative to Earthbound Lines," *Internet World,* March 9, 1998: 45.

42 *"It is, after all, just sand"* Nicholas Negroponte, *Being Digital* (New York: Alfred A. Knopf, 1995), 23.

42 *As a general rule* Eric Schmidt's comments here are from his August 29, 1998, conversation with Tad Tuleja.

43 *In a speech to industry leaders* Eric Schmidt, "The Evolution of Networking," *Computer Reseller News,* December 1, 1997: 154–56.

45 *"cookies"* For Olivo's and other concerns about cookies, see Chip Bayers, "The Promise of One to One: A Love Story," *Wired,* May 1998: 184.

46 *Bronti Kelly* His story is told in Will Rodger, "Lives Online: Cyberspace's Identity Crisis," *Interactive Week,* December 1, 1997: 52–53.

48 *If a hacker can penetrate the Pentagon* For a disturbing account of breached Pentagon security, see Mike Brunker, "Hackers penetrate Pentagon network," MSNBC News, April 21, 1998. It is available online at *www.msnbc.com/news.*

53 *"good-faith dialogue"* Barry Smith is quoted in Will Rodger, "In Reversal, FBI Drops Encryption Demands," *Interactive Week,* March 23, 1998.

59 *"dramatic increase"* Cyndy Ainsworth is quoted in Sharon Machlis, "More Put Credit Cards Online," *Computerworld,* March 16, 1998: 6.

59 *Indiscriminate blasting* John White's comments come from his September 2, 1998, conversation with Tad Tuleja.

62 *"immature and ornery"* See the Test Center Analysis on network security auditing in *InfoWorld,* March 16, 1998: 54.

63 *As for outsourcing* See Todd Spangler, "IBM Launches New Array

of Security Consulting Services," *Internet World,* April 6, 1998: 26; and Joel Scambray, "Outsourcing Your Security Problems," *InfoWorld,* March 16, 1998: 62.

63 *"Information is power"* Deborah Radcliff, "Is Your ISP Secure?" *InfoWorld,* March 2, 1998: 97.

Chapter 3: Lessons of the First Generation

68 *the "directing traffic" mix* For a good summary of the options here, see Bruce Judson, *Net Marketing* (New York: Wolff New Media, 1996), 91–119.

72 *The Preview deal* Information on this and the other deals mentioned here comes from Bill Roberts, "Intuit to Pay $30M to Put Content on AOL's Online Service, Web Site." *Internet World,* February 23, 1998: 4.

73 *"positive impact on intent to purchase"* The Millward Brown Interactive study is cited in *www.tenagra-awards-list@awards.tenagra.com.*

74 *"clickitis"* The term was coined by Chuck Martin in *The Digital Estate: Strategies for Competing, Surviving, and Thriving in an Internetworked World* (New York: McGraw-Hill, 1997), 64.

74 *"thick description"* See Clifford Geertz, "Thick Description: Toward an Interpretive Theory of Culture," in *The Interpretation of Cultures* (New York: Basic Books, 1973), 7.

77 *The most effective Web sites* Evan I. Schwartz, *Webonomics: Nine Essential Principles for Growing Your Business on the World Wide Web* (New York: Broadway Books, 1997), 25.

78 *Logos* The company is profiled in Bruno Giussani, "With Net, Italian Translation Company Reshapes Itself for the Information Age," *New York Times* on the Web, April 15, 1997.

79 *Starwave* See the profile in James Oliver Cury, "Making Money Online," Austin/San Antonio *Computer Currents,* May 1998: 16–18; and Schwartz, *Webonomics,* 36.

82 *the three-click rule* One of Chuck Martin's 100 rules of business "Netiquette." See *Digital Estate*, 197.

83 " *'Nice Web site, but'* " See Schwartz, *Webonomics*, 48.

84 *Daniel Leemon* The Schwab executive's comments are from an interview conducted on August 24, 1998, by Pat House.

86 *"virtual integration"* See, for example, Matt Krantz, "New Alliances Lining Up 'Virtually,' Not Vertically," *Investor's Business Daily*, April 20, 1998: A8.

87 *Keith Krach* His comment appears in Mel Duvall's story on Ariba, "Partnerships Boost E-Com Effort," *Interactive Week*, March 30, 1998: 14.

87 *Classifieds2000* For a story on this company, including the comments of Karim El-Fishawy, see Susan Dumett, "It's Classified and On-line," Microsoft's *Internet Magazine*, April 6–12, 1998.

88 *"launch and learn"* Martin, *Digital Estate*, 13–16.

89 *Russ Gillam* His comments appear in John Evan Frook's profile of the Disney site, "Disney Tempts Web Visitors to Buy," *InternetWeek*, March 23, 1998.

93 *Pete Solvik* The Cisco chief information officer was interviewed in January 1998 by Ronald McElhaney.

94 *John Chambers* See his keynote speech to the 1997 Comdex conference, reported as "Preparing for an Evolution," in *Computer Reseller News*, December 1, 1997: 148.

Chapter 4: Private "Infotainment" Will Give Way to Global
   Enterprise

97 *"Future Schlock"* The Postman attack is cited in Don Tapscott, *The Digital Economy* (New York: McGraw-Hill, 1996), 73.

99 *"obvious" addresses turn up surprises* The examples given here come from Bruce Judson, *Net Marketing* (New York: Wolff New Media, 1996), 42–43.

99 *PETA* The case is discussed in Matt Richtel, "You Can't Always Judge a Domain by Its Name," *New York Times,* May 28, 1998.

101 *"We get it"* See "Europe's Internet Growth," a Forrester Report by Joe Sawyer, Emily Nagle Green, and Sarah Gerber, vol. 1, no. 1, April 1998, available at *www.forrester.com.*

103 *PlanetAll* Company president Warren Adams was interviewed in August 1998, by Salman Malik and Tad Tuleja.

114 *Making Entertainment Pay* See "Internet Games," a Forrester Report by Seema Chowdhury, William M. Bluestein, and Kara S. Davis, vol. 1, no. 1, April 1, 1997, available at *www.forrester.com.*

115 *Rules and No Rules* Professor Joe Lassiter was interviewed on September 2, 1998, by Salman Malik and Tad Tuleja.

Chapter 5: Internet Pioneers Will Reshape Their Industries

121 *Tickets Plus* Information on Preview Travel, including the quotations from its president and CEO, Ken Orton, comes from James Oliver Cury's excellent profile in "Making Money Online," Austin/San Antonio *Computer Currents,* May 1998: 15.

125 *Top 200* The *Net Marketing* choices may be found at *www.netb2b.com.*

125 *What makes Dell stand out* Dell's success, and the comments of manager Bill Morris, are recorded well in Cury, "Making Money Online," 15–16.

127 *Amazon has truly transformed* Professor Joe Lassiter's comments in this chapter come from his September 2, 1998, interview with Salman Malik and Tad Tuleja.

Chapter 6: Market Models Will Multiply, Not Contract

132 *Eric Schmidt* His comments in this chapter are from his August 29, 1998, interview with Tad Tuleja.

137 *Concurring with Eric's assessment* John White's comments are from his September 2, 1998, interview with Tad Tuleja.

143 *Ira Motor Group* Information on this company, including Bob Staretz's comments, comes from John Fontana, "Dealer Cuts Costs with Web Kiosks," *InternetWeek*, March 2, 1998, online at *pubs.cmpnet.com/internetwk*.

144 *Charles Schwab* Daniel Leemon's comments are from an August 24, 1998, interview with Pat House.

147 *supply "webs"* For supply webs, including James Skinner's comments, see Neil Gross, "Leapfrogging a Few Links," *Business Week*, June 22, 1998: 140–42.

Chapter 7: Online Companies Will Become Para-Enterprises

149 *the business-to-business market* The marketing director is quoted in Mel Duvall, "Businesses Buy Into E-Commerce," *Interactive Week*, February 2, 1998: 33.

150 *"communities of commerce"* The quoted material comes from Sharon McDonnell, "Big Growth Seen in Business-to-Business Sites," *New York Times* on the Web, March 8, 1997.

151 *one Internet consultant* Maxine Martell, president of Martell Consulting, quoted ibid.

156 *GartnerGroup VP* Vinnie Mirchandani talked to reporters Neil Gross and Ira Sager for their article "Caution Signs along the Road," *Business Week*, June 22, 1998: 168.

158 *Driving efficiencies at MCI-Worldcom* Mike Betzer's comments come from his October 1, 1998, interview with Tad Tuleja.

160 *Floating Titanic* The information on *Titanic,* including the quoted material, is from John Madden, "Keeping 'Titanic' Afloat," *PC Week,* April 6, 1998: 27.

164 *Savings from this first step alone* Estimates by Forrester Research

analyst Steven Ball, cited in Carol Sliwa, " 'Net Used to Extend EDI's Reach," *Computerworld,* February 23, 1998: 1.

166 *The Compaq Example* John White's comments are from his September 2, 1998, interview with Tad Tuleja.

170 *By 2003* The estimate is cited in Andy Reinhardt, "Log On, Link Up, Save Big," *Business Week,* June 22, 1998: 138.

170 *A boxmaker* For the Genstar story, see Natalie Engler, "The Second Coming of Electronic Commerce," *Computerworld Emmerce,* December 15, 1997: 14–15.

171 *One-stop shopping* For the L.A. County story, see Reinhardt, "Log On," 132.

172 *"Fast or forgotten"* Ibid., 134–35.

172 *Virtual conferencing* See Anne Zeiger, "Marketing Firm Makes Rooms for Clients," *InternetWeek,* February 2, 1998, at *http://pubs. cmpnet.com/internetwk/case/study0202-3*

173 *Bringing It All Together* Pete Solvik's comments in this section come from an interview conducted by Ronald McElhaney in January 1998.

177 *The company's CEO* John Chambers's keynote speech to the 1997 Comdex conference was reported as "Preparing for an Evolution," in *Computer Reseller News,* December 1, 1997: 146.

Chapter 8: The Net Will Move from Communities to "Customerization"

182 *Community Knowledge* See Chuck Don Peppers and Martha Rogers, *Enterprise One to One: Tools for Competing in the Interactive Age* (New York: Doubleday, 1997), 231.

183 *DoubleClick* See Chuck Martin, *The Digital Estate: Strategies for Competing, Surviving, and Thriving in an Internetworked World* (New York: McGraw-Hill, 1997), 119–23.

185 *Profiles are updated on the fly* Press release on the 1997 Annual

Tenagra Awards for Internet Marketing Excellence, e-mailed to *www.tenagra-awards-list@awards.tenagra.com.*

187 *"The more a company can deliver"* Stanley M. Davis, *Future Perfect* (Reading, MA: Addison-Wesley, 1987), 157.

187 *"economies of scope"* B. Joseph Pine II, *Mass Customization: The New Frontier in Business Competition* (Boston: Harvard Business School Press, 1993), 48–49.

188 *Toyota now invites* For the Toyota and other stories cited here, see ibid., 36–42, 175–76.

188 *"markets of one"* See Peppers and Rogers, *Enterprise One to One.*

189 *Customizing for Individuals and Enterprises* John White was interviewed on September 2, 1998, by Tad Tuleja.

192 *Another View of Profiling* Eric Schmidt was interviewed on August 29, 1998, by Tad Tuleja.

197 *A Final Word: The Schwab Experience* Daniel Leemon was interviewed on August 24, 1998, by Pat House.

Chapter 9: The Sales and Marketing Landscape Will Be Redrawn

200 *Virtual Middlemen* For information on "vortex" businesses, and specifically on Realbid, see Kevin Jones, "Vortex Businesses Find Vitality on the Net," *Interactive Week,* March 23, 1998: 60.

201 *Reliance* For this story, including the customer testimonial, see Bob Dorf, "The One-to-One Insurance Policy," *Inside 1to1,* available online at *PeppersAndRogers@1to1.com,* April 16, 1998.

202 *Electronic Gavel Wielders* For the electronic auction trend, see Howard Millman, "Online Auctions Are Changing the Face of Retail Landscape," *InfoWorld,* March 9, 1998: 77; and Saul Hansell, "Hackers' Bazaar," *New York Times,* April 2, 1998: D1.

207 *If a company succeeds* Jim Dickie's comments here come from his article "The Death of Sales Force Automation," *Siebel Magazine,* vol. 2, no. 1, p. 48.

208 *"win-win for current customers"* See Pat House, "Siebel Systems Successfully Completes Merger with Scopus Technology," *Siebel Magazine,* vol. 2, no. 1, p. 9.

209 *Beyond "Sneakernet" at Firefly* Salman Malik's comments come from an interview with Tad Tuleja on September 11, 1998.

212 *By the time you've interactively customized* Thomas M. Siebel and Michael S. Malone, *Virtual Selling* (New York: Free Press, 1996), 198.

213 *"gargantuan piles of infotrash"* See Howard Millman, "Agents at Your Service," *InfoWorld,* February 16, 1998: 77.

215 *The View from MCI-Worldcom* Mike Betzer's comments are from his October 1, 1998, interview with Tad Tuleja.

Chapter 11: Rolling It Out II: Nuts and Bolts

242 *Bill Kilday* All further comments from Bill Kilday in this chapter are drawn from an interview with Tad Tuleja on June 24, 1998.

243 *Step One: Finding an ISP* The following discussion draws on James Michael Stewart's excellent article "Is Your ISP a Good Fit?" in Austin/San Antonio *Computer Currents,* June 1998: 15–20. The monthly is also available on-line at *www.currents.net/austin.*

244 *Boardwatch Magazine study* See also Randy Barrett, "Peering into the Future: Private Exchanges Win," *Interactive Week,* February 8, 1998: 8.

246 *Gargoyles* See Joe Mullich, "Sunglass Maker Says Epoch Delivers Clear View of Web Technology," *InternetWeek,* December 15, 1997. At *http://pubs.cmpnet.com/internetwk/case/study1215-3.htm.*

248 *revised naming system* See Bridget Mintz Testa, "Domain Name Update," *Current Technology,* April 1998: 31–32.

249 *"Real Name" search process* See Elizabeth Gardner, "Deal Allows Companies to Buy Top Spot in Search Results," *Internet World,* May 18, 1998: 54.

250 *Ted Finch* His comments in this chapter come from an interview with Tad Tuleja on June 1, 1998.

254 *Step Four: Managing the Site* Information on Webmasters in this section comes from Charles Babcock, "The World Wide Web Gets Down to Business," *Interactive Week,* March 2, 1998: 20–22.

255 *CustomerSat.com survey* Ibid.

258 *Much of the return* The savings estimate is by Cisco CEO John Chambers, cited in Andy Reinhardt, "Log On, Link Up, Save Big," *Business Week,* June 22, 1998: 134.

258 *International Data Corporation* The survey was reported in Mark Halper, "So, Does Your Web Site Pay?" *Forbes ASAP,* August 25, 1997. At *www.forbes.com/asap/97/0825/117.htm.*

259 *Ticketmaster* Ibid.

261 *Millipore Corporation* For the Millipore story, see Carla Catalano, "For a Pleasing Commerce Site . . . Look, Listen, Ask and Respond," *Computerworld Emmerce,* March 8, 1998: 6.

262 *Successful customer service always means* From Jim Sterne, *Customer Service on the Internet: Building Relationships, Increasing Loyalty, Staying Competitive* (New York: John Wiley & Sons, 1996).

Index